THE RETURN OF MERITOCRACY

Conservative Ideas for Unlocking Social Mobility

THE RETURN OF MERITOCRACY

Conservative Ideas for Unlocking Social Mobility

PAUL MAGINNIS

PME

PUBLISHING

Published by PME Publishing

A CIP catalogue record for this book is available from the British Library.

ISBN 978-1-9999540-0-0

Book layout and design by Clare Brayshaw

Prepared and printed by:

York Publishing Services Ltd
64 Hallfield Road
Layerthorpe
York YO31 7ZQ

Tel: 01904 431213

Website: www.yps-publishing.co.uk

Contents

Introduction

I felt incredibly relieved when I first moved from Northern Ireland to Sheffield back in 2010. Mainly to get away from the sectarian politics which I had grown up with but I also wanted to delve into the 'big issues' of the day such as the economy, inequality and the new Coalition Government. Of course, as any self-respecting 18-year-old from a low income background, I considered myself to be a socialist. How could I be anything else?

From what I remember, I first considered myself a socialist towards the end of sixth form. By the time I started university I thought what we needed was a revolution to bring the entire system down. I remember talking to my friends both in sixth form and at university arrogantly pontificating about how any decent human being could ever vote Conservative. Needless to say this point of view was widespread amongst nearly all student colleagues and without a doubt amongst all university lecturers who taught me.

If you speak to the average young person, they will often use the same words when describing the Conservatives. 'Arrogant', 'elitist' and 'nasty' are the three words which usually come up in conversation when discussing the Conservatives. At university, most students live in a bubble and a groupthink mainstream opinion in being left-wing is standard. But even though I despised the Tories, I wanted to learn more about the Party to really take the fight to them. I bought a book on Margaret Thatcher, a book on Conservative

Ideology and I paid a lot of attention to arguments regarding Conservative values and policies by engrossing myself in shows like *The Daily Politics* and *Newsnight*. Within weeks of swatting up on political knowledge to take the argument to my opponents, frightfully strange thoughts began to occur.

A month or two after starting university, the scales began to fall from my eyes. I realised that socialism was not the answer as it was the politics of envy, the politics of protest and the belief in attacking aspirations and promoting equality of outcome. I realised it was the values of responsibility, freedom of the individual and equality of opportunity which I truly believed in. My damascene conversion hit home as what the Conservatives were arguing struck a deep chord within me.

Looking back, it was clear that I was always going to be Conservative. I was raised in a single-parent household for the vast majority of my childhood and my mum always drummed into me values of self-reliance, work ethic and living within your means. She always taught my siblings and I not to spend money we didn't have and to manage our budgets accordingly. With values such as this and with the Coalition Government determined to tackle the inherited budget deficit of £150 billion a year, how could I not be a Conservative?

I had my first paper round when I was 12 and began working at McDonald's when I was 16. Work ethic and self-reliance was something instilled into me, especially as some members of my family were on long-term welfare. This background meant I was a true believer in the government's radical social security reforms but this had to be intertwined with the influential Conservative ideas of opportunity and aspiration. Equality of opportunity is what I truly believed in, not equality of outcome. I realised that socialists can never believe in aspiration because this pursuit inevitably creates inequality, which they fundamentally oppose. After establishing my true values how could I not be a Conservative?

By the end of 2010, I was arguing against the university establishment and at the same time being seen by peers as arguing *for* the political establishment. After some years of confusion, before my 19th birthday I was an open supporter of the Conservative Party. What was clear to me was the fact that I was not born into the Tory Party, I chose it through thinking deeply about my values, completing independent research and not giving way to university groupthink pressures.

Since failing my 11 Plus in 2003 and therefore attending a poor performing secondary modern school, the concept of social mobility has always fascinated me. How can we help those from the poorest backgrounds move up the social ladder? How can we ensure that those who do attend low performing schools have the opportunity to move up the social ladder? I want to live in a society where an individual's hard work and talent is the judge of how far they get in life and this is my true political passion. This is why I have worked in a variety of jobs that are about helping people who are struggling and to empower them to reach their full potential.

I have spent my short career in roles such as a homelessness support worker and advocating for children in care. But again, many on the Left who dominate these jobs believe the answer is paying more money in welfare or simply throwing money at children in care to make up for their lack of family life. In jobs working with the disadvantaged, I've always promoted aspiration, work ethic and creating a strong family, not reliance on state subsidies as a long-term solution. Helping the most disadvantaged in society is seen as a 'left-wing' thing to do. I want to show in this book that the Left do not have a monopoly on social justice.

Several years ago John Major was asked on a Radio 4 programme why he chose the Conservatives.[1] Why would somebody born in poverty from a working-class estate in Brixton become a Conservative? Why would somebody who

1 *Reflections with Peter Hennessy*, BBC Radio 4, 13th August 2014.

grew up sharing two bedrooms with five people become a Conservative? Why would somebody who left school at 15 and even got rejected as a bus conductor become a Conservative? Major's response to this was fascinating. He described how the local Labour Party asked people to stay where they were, be patient and in due course they would help them. Conversely, the Conservatives said they would like to open up avenues of opportunity for you to change your own circumstances. Major stated he was by instinct a Conservative and his answer to the above question showed it was partly to do with social mobility.

Rags to riches stories have become even less likely in twenty-first century Britain than it was when John Major was growing up. There are many fiercely disputed reasons for the decline in social mobility, from changes in the economy to education reforms. Throughout this book, I will identify and analyse many of these contributing factors. It is always easier to stand on the side-lines and be critical of any governments policies, it's much more difficult to come up with practical positive solutions, which I intend to do.

In each chapter under the 'Moving Forward' section, I propose policies which aim to promote a more meritocratic society, but in a radically Tory way. In improving the Conservative Party's image, I will write about ideas such as building a mass membership and making the Conservatives look more like the country it seeks to represent. The chapter on the economy focuses on closing the budget deficit and defending capitalism but at the same time reforming it and reducing 'unfair inequalities'. In education I seek to detail ways to improve our schools so they produce better outcomes for the poorest students whilst also discussing alternatives to tuition fees. When it comes to family and community I will unashamedly promote strong two-parent families and consider ways to increase social action in society. In the welfare chapter I will make a defence of social security but advocate for a contribution based system moving forward. I will then critique socialism and clearly show that as they support equality of outcome, it is diametrically opposed to a meritocratic society. Finally, I conclude with how the Conservatives can win the '2020 General Election' through introducing long lasting radical policies which dramatically increase social mobility in Britain.

There are many vital issues which this country is currently grappling with. From Brexit, to terrorism, to funding our NHS, the country faces monumental challenges. But I am dismayed with the media's lack of focus on social mobility. This book will partly be a recent history of the last seven years, but will also attempt to contribute to the debate moving forward into the next decade. As well as analysing the governments record I want to include stories from my personal and work life. I hope this mixture of anecdotal and empirical evidence will make it readable to many who follow politics to varying degrees.

This book is not exhaustive and will focus on selected themes. Some analyses are longer than others and some ideas that I've developed are more detailed than others. It takes a range of policy areas from across government in the hope to promote ideas which help social mobility. The main reason I wrote this book is because I am a firm believer that it is Conservative thinking which has the solutions to the big questions and it is only the Conservatives who can create a more socially mobile society through opening up opportunities. With the disaster of the 2017 General Election, I feel new ideas are needed from the grassroots to contribute to the debate in the coming years. What I want to show in this book is that there are clear policy choices available to once again make people feel proud about voting Conservative.

1 Improving the Brand

> *"There's a lot we need to do in this party of ours. Our base is too narrow and so, occasionally, are our sympathies. You know what some people call us: the nasty party."*[2]
>
> *– Theresa May, 2002*

Introduction

Several years ago I was standing in the smoking area of a pub in Sheffield talking to a few friends of mine about party politics. They were all on the Left of the political persuasion so I enjoyed challenging their assumptions about their views of the centre Right. I started asking them a series of questions in relation to political policies and whether or not they agreed if they were good ideas. Some of the policies I queried them on included tax cuts for the lowest earners, extra money in schools for the most disadvantaged pupils and a family intervention programme which would help the most problematic families find work. My friends were in absolute agreement with me and repeated their favourite phrases like "You're my favourite Tory" or "You aren't really a Conservative stating these sorts of policies". I delightedly informed them that these were not my ideas but they were being implemented by the Conservative-led government at that very moment.

2 Theresa May, Conservative Party Conference, 7th October 2002.

On reflection of discussions like this, it both pleases and worries me that the aforementioned policies are not seen as Conservative policies. It pleases me that many of the policies which tackle injustices in Britain are seen as fundamentally right; it is worrying that they are seen as non-Conservative. It isn't just the usual Corbynista types who believe this about the Conservatives but many centre ground voters as well. The majority of centre ground voters agree with Conservative policies in most areas of the economy and society, but they are suspicious of our instincts and our values.

In the forthcoming chapters, I intend to set out how the Conservative Party can implement policies in a variety of areas which can make the United Kingdom a more just society with upward mobility at its heart. However, before non-Tory voters can be expected to vote for us, we need to tackle the Party's image problem and let ordinary people know we are on their side. Brand is just as vital in politics as it is in business. Those in business value the importance of a brand just as highly as the contents. This illustrates that both perception and reality are deeply interlinked.

Much of this chapter will focus on the negative perception members of the public have of the Conservative Party and I will raise what I believe to be genuinely fair criticisms throughout. I intend to tackle the Thatcher and immediate post-Thatcher Conservative Party's views on social justice issues, with a particular focus on social mobility. I will then analyse David Cameron's 'modernising' programme in Opposition and how this was influenced by being in a government with an out of control budget deficit. I will finish with my thoughts on the 2017 General Election and discuss ideas for improving the brand in relation to image, policies and renewing the dwindling Tory membership.

Modern Historical Context

Growing up in Northern Ireland at the time of the Peace Process and with a new devolved assembly at Stormont, I was naturally interested in politics. From a very young age I remember developing a thirst for understanding British politics, that's what fascinated me the most. When the main political parties were being described to me, I was always told 'the Conservatives are the party for rich people, not people like us'. Many years later at the age of 18, when I considered myself a socialist, I recall arrogantly sitting in my A Level politics classes and attacking the Conservatives in a grotesquely envious and classist way. This sort of hateful ignorance which my younger self portrayed is unfortunately all too common in 2017.

I grew up with the legacy of Margaret Thatcher still being pertinent within the Conservative Party. She was undoubtedly a fantastic prime minister in the way she revitalised and revolutionised the economy. The way she told the IRA 'crime is crime', the way she rescued the Falkland Islands and in the way she finally answered Heath's question 'who governs Britain?' when it came to the unions.

Thatcher was deemed by many as a champion for opportunity and aspiration. Letting council house tenants buy their own home drastically improved social mobility, nearly doubling home ownership in Britain within a decade. Ironically, this policy was the biggest redistribution of wealth from the government to the people in the post-war era. Thatcher created a 'share owning democracy' where amazingly more people owned shares from the privatised industries than there were members of trade unions.

Although Margaret Thatcher was a great advocate for social mobility (her own background as a grocer's daughter helps legitimise this claim), she was not always considered an advocate for social justice. The great council house sale which helped so many working-class people 'get on in life' was fantastic for that generation, but the unwillingness of successive governments to build replacement homes has been disastrous. With many council houses sold off and not being replaced, decades later this has led to a chronic shortage for the descendants of this generation.

Another example of Thatcher being seen as lacking in compassion was the closing of much of British industry which led to over 3 million people out of work. I don't disagree that the mines had to be closed as they were inefficient and increasingly archaic, but the tone during these closures and lack of retraining schemes for good working-class men was deeply regretful. Furthermore, the poll tax (a flat tax paid by everybody no matter how much their wealth or income) was another policy seen to be unfair by the British public and still hasn't been forgotten by many voters. Although interestingly the BBC licence fee has never raised the same level of public anger, when logically it's just as regressive as the poll tax.

Following on from Thatcher's Government, John Major's time as prime minister was a missed opportunity in promoting the Conservative Party as the 'socially just' political party in Britain. Major's extraordinary achievement of becoming the first working-class post-war prime minster should have led the public to believe that the Conservatives were the party of social mobility. A man who left school at 15 and didn't go to university managed to become the leader of the Conservative Party. Despite this, the Party's entrenched image as 'the nasty party' had already taken hold and bitter infighting within the government meant Major never managed to make inroads on promoting a socially just society in which he clearly believed. In later years he openly stated that he regretted not doing more to promote social mobility through the education system.[3]

The opposition years between 1997–2010 were a long, often painful journey for the Conservatives, as the Party

3 John Major speech, South Norfolk Conservative Association, November 2013.

attempted to rebuild itself after the crushing defeat by New Labour. All three leaders, William Hague, Iain Duncan Smith and Michael Howard, struggled against Tony Blair as they failed to attract electors from outside the core vote. After 18 years of Conservative rule, the Party was tired, split and devoid of a coherent unified theme. All three began their leadership by attempting to put their own footprint on the Party but had to resort to their core vote when pressure began to mount as no progress had been made against New Labour's electoral success.

The previously mentioned criticisms created a somewhat unfair perception of the Conservatives. Throughout the 18 years of Tory Government, there were some great achievements which focused on helping lower and middle income people get on in life. The privatisation of industry, tax cutting and reform of the trade unions meant Britain became a dynamic economy once more. Thatcher's policies were so powerful it led to a new consensus as Tony Blair adopted much of her economic policies.

To some extent, the Major Government also helped many ordinary taxpayers by shifting the burden of tax from income to consumption. Additionally, the Conservatives showed their belief in promoting social mobility as the Party had a state schooled leader for 40 years between 1965–2005. This challenges the unfair assumption that the Conservatives are 'elitist' and 'out of touch'. After four decades of state-schooled leaders, this came to an end when David Cameron was elected as leader of the Conservatives in December 2005.

Cameron Modernisation 2005–10

David Cameron should be recognised as the first Conservative leader to understand that there was a serious image problem for the Party in the post-Thatcher era. Even though an old Etonian, he was determined to prove that it was not about 'where you are from but where you are going'. Cameron sought to implement liberal conservatism and it was his mission to show the Conservative Party could be comfortable with modern Britain. Cameron was on the same page as Theresa May when she declared 'some people call us the nasty party', in her 2002 conference speech.[4] Cameron intended to 'detoxify' the Tory brand in Opposition, by changing the Party's grassroots opinions, tone and policy direction. He endeavoured to put issues like social justice and social mobility at the forefront of his strategy.

Cameron's first objective after being elected as leader of the Conservatives was to change the Party internally. Even after eight years in Opposition, the Conservatives had made no progress in tackling its core weaknesses, that is, being perceived as too white, elitist and male. The evidence for this seems overwhelming. In 2005, out of a Parliamentary Party of 197, the Conservatives had 17 women (9% of total), 2 ethnic-minority candidates (1% of total) but managed to have 15 Etonions (8% of total). Cameron aimed to rectify this by adopting an 'A-List' of priority candidates for the 2010 General Election. Over half this list included women and many ethnic-minority candidates. This was a serious effort by Cameron to change the face of the Parliamentary Party and he used the MPs' expenses scandal to help accelerate the modernisation process.

By 2010, Cameron could claim to be successful in changing the Conservatives as there was a substantial improvement when it came to more women and ethnic minorities being elected to parliament. Following the 2010 election there were 49 Conservative woman MPs (16% of total). Feminists constantly lament how dreadful it is that there are not enough women MPs, however this election showed positive progress for the Conservatives as this counted for a 190% increase in women MPs from the 2005 parliament.

4 Ibid 2.

In addition to this, 11 ethnic-minority candidates were elected in 2010 (4% of total). This was another fantastic improvement and illustrated the positive direction that the Party was going in. Although, regrettably the Conservatives only received 16% of the ethnic-minority vote in 2010 and this reflected the fact that many minorities deemed the Conservatives as openly hostile to their values.

Both these increases have certainly helped the Conservatives look more like the country it seeks to represent. The A-List's record on getting more state-schooled Conservatives into parliament is more mixed. Overall, the number of private-schooled Conservatives fell from 60% in 2005 to 54% in 2010. Although it is encouraging that more state-schooled Conservatives entered parliament, the number of Etonions increased from 15 to 20. There is nothing wrong in principle that people from Eton want to dedicate themselves to public service, but when so many are in parliament it does make the public suspicious of the 'old boys' network'.

Having changed the internal structures and tackled the lack of diversity within the Party, Cameron combined this with a change in vision and in policies. This change in vision began with Cameron's party conference speech in October 2006, in which he proclaimed that 'the centre ground is where you will find the dreams of most people in this country'.[5] Cameron intended to make the Conservatives seem more liberal, compassionate and fitting for a twenty-first-century Britain. From the get go as leader he declared 'let sunshine win the day' and wished to be seen as optimistic by his Party and his country.

In Opposition, Cameron focused on setting out an agenda which intended to change the public persona of the Conservatives. For Cameron, 2006 was an important year for building his reputation as a different type of Tory leader.

5 David Cameron, Conservative Party Conference, 4th October 2006.

He sought to change the Party's views, both socially and economically. In July 2006, Cameron made a now infamous speech on crime and family breakdown. During the so called 'hug a hoodie' speech,[6] Cameron showed that he could be 'tough on the causes of crime', as well as crime itself. This was a world away from the 1990s' rhetoric of his former mentor and boss Michael Howard who was a firm believer in prison for offenders.

At the conference in October 2006, Cameron told the Conservatives to 'stop banging on about Europe and tax cuts'.[7] This was a bold statement to bring the Conservatives onto Labour's centre ground of pro-Europeanism and showed a firm stance in unfunded tax cuts. In terms of public spending, in 2007 George Osborne matched Labour's spending pledges. This showed an economic shift to Labour's territory of high government spending and high taxes.

On gay rights David Cameron regretted Section 28[8] and in 2009 apologised for the Conservatives offending gay people.[9] This focus on being socially and economically liberal was designed to attract many New Labour and Liberal Democrat voters. Although David Cameron's modernisation was deemed by many as being essential to improving the Tory brand, he managed to alienate many on the political Right and at the same time he did not manage to convince enough centrist voters that the Conservatives had sufficiently changed.

At the 2010 election, the Conservatives were the largest party but 19 short of a majority. Even with the Party's rightful declaration that this was the largest amount of Tory seats gained at an election since 1931, it was a monumental

---

6 David Cameron Speech, Centre for Social Justice, 10th July 2006.

7 Ibid 5.

8 Local Government Act 1988, Section 28.

9 http://www.telegraph.co.uk/news/politics/david-cameron/5710650/David-Cameron-says-sorry-over-Section-28-gay-law.html [Accessed 17th February 2017]

disappointment. I urge the reader to take a step back and remember just how unpopular Gordon Brown's Government was. An example of this was at the 2009 European Election when the Labour Party got 15.7% of the vote. This was the first time in British history that a party in government had been outpolled in a national election by a party with no representation in the House of Commons (UKIP).

In 2010, the Conservatives were up against a discredited, divided and dishevelled Labour leadership. A party which had been in power for 13 years and were widely deemed economically incompetent after the financial crash. To top this off during the election campaign, Brown labelled one of Labour's own voters a bigot after being friendly to her face. Despite all this, the Conservatives were still not trusted enough by the electorate to win a majority in 2010.

The failure of the Conservatives to win a majority can be traced back to the beginning of Cameron's premiership. Cameron called UKIP voters a bunch of 'fruitcakes, loonies and closet racists'.[10] This was just as offensive to many Conservative backbenchers in his own party. At the time, many on the centre Right of politics were not interested in 'hugging a hoodie' but wanted a hoodie to be locked up if they hurt somebody or burgled a person's house. They did not want to be told to 'stop banging on about Europe' when they had genuine concerns about sovereignty and immigration control.

Most Conservatives would rather have seen more emphasis on core issues like Europe or tax cuts rather than climate change and matching Labour's bloated public spending. Cameron managed to alienate the core vote further when he declared himself the 'heir to Blair'.[11] The majority of Conservatives were certainly uncomfortable with their leader

10 *LBC*, 2006.

11 Andrew Pierce, *The Times*, 5th October 2005, 'Horror as Cameron brandishes the B-word'.

preferring to be compared to Tony Blair rather than Margaret Thatcher. Additionally, many commentators thought that much of the Cameron rebranding was spin. After the 2010 General Election, it was clear that David Cameron had a long way to go in detoxifying the Tory brand.

Cameron in Government 2010–16

As Cameron fell short of a majority government following the 2010 General Election, he called for a 'big, bold and comprehensive' deal with the Liberal Democrats. With the country facing colossal difficulties, the Conservative leadership sought to rely on the 57 Liberal Democrat MPs to be a shield for the most difficult decisions. The centre ground, Orange Book[12] liberals had taken charge of the Liberal Democrats and believed in many of the same policies as a modernised Conservative Party.

The Coalition Agreement set out a wide range of policies, many of which would have an impact on social mobility, e.g. tax, education and welfare reform. The Coalition took on the mammoth task of attempting to improve social mobility in the age of austerity. This was a genuinely new politics and the Conservatives were determined to show that they could work with a moderate Liberal Democrat Party.

Throughout the five years of the Coalition Government, there were many setbacks when it came to the public's perception of the Conservative Party. Much of this was unfair but clearly a large proportion of the public still perceived the Party to be 'out of touch' and 'elitist'. To begin with, the Coalition Government was accused by the *Daily Mail* of being a 'coalition of millionaires'.[13] They revealed that 23

12 Paul Marshall and David Laws, *The Orange Book: Reclaiming Liberalism*, Profile Books Ltd, 2004.

13 http://www.dailymail.co.uk/news/election/article-1280554/The-coalition-millionaires-23-29-member-new-cabinet-worth-1m--Lib-Dems-just-wealthy-Tories.html [Accessed 18th February 2017]

out of the 29 cabinet ministers in Cameron's first government were worth over £1 million.

There were plenty of examples which led the public to believe that the Tories were out of touch. George Osborne was central to this perception and his Budgets will be examined later in this chapter and detailed further in Chapter 2. Enhancing the Tory brand, whilst implementing austerity was always going to be a challenge. Over the years I have spoken to people who should be potential Tory voters and it is clear that they perceived George Osborne's Budgets as grossly unfair. In the 2010 Budget, VAT was raised from 17.5% to 20% and with living standards stagnating at best, this was seen as a regressive move by many lower and middle income families. The 2012 Budget was named the 'omnishambles' Budget as the Coalition reduced the higher rate of income tax from 50p to 45p whilst seemingly introducing the 'pasty tax', 'caravan tax' and the 'granny tax'.

The 2012 Budget damaged the reputation of the Conservatives, however cutting Tax Credits after the 2015 General Election had an even bigger detrimental impact on the Party. This policy contradicted the Party's rhetoric of being on the side of people who want to work hard and get on. There was of course, a dramatic U-turn on the Tax Credit cuts which would no longer be implemented until the living wage, further personal allowance increases and free childcare had all come into force.

Throughout Osborne's Budgets, corporation tax was slashed from 28% to 19% which led to protestations on the Left believing that the Conservatives were only concerned about the interests of the rich and powerful. Was this perception of Osborne fair? I am a firm believer that overall Osborne did a good job as Chancellor but some of his decisions were clearly questionable at best. In terms of Osborne's tax and spending policies, I will delve into them in further detail in the next chapter. This chapter focuses on image so let me now argue the case that much of the public's perceptions of Osborne as an 'out of touch' 'poor bashing' Chancellor is grossly unjustified. Osborne's most notable achievement when it came to tax reform was not the cutting of the higher rate tax, but the lifting of the personal allowance from £6,475 in 2010 to £11,000 by 2016. This was a tax cut worth £905 a year to all lower and middle income earners.

Other policies which helped aspirational lower to middle earners was cutting stamp duty at the lower end of the market and raising it for the richest, helping the lowest income earners with free childcare and of course the living wage, implemented in the 2015 Budget. He targeted the better off with many tax rises including dividends tax, restrictions in Child Benefit for higher rate taxpayers and the bank levy. I will go into further detail regarding Osborne's tax and spending policies on the richest and poorest households in the next chapter but the idea that he did not target the better off through the tax system is simply untrue. Admittedly this is not how the public perceived him and several of his Budgets were PR disasters.

Alongside economics, Cameron sought to show that he was a socially progressive Conservative leader. First and foremost, this came in his victorious leadership speech in December 2005. He proclaimed that "There is such thing as society; it's just not the same as the State".[14] Cameron was a true believer in the Big Society and much of this idea had substance, e.g. Free Schools, National Citizen Service and the devolution to cities were all part of the Big Society. I will explore this idea later in this book but once again the idea was not sold to the public in the correct way.

The public still don't understand what the term Big Society means and it was allowed to be manipulated by the Left who claimed it was an excuse to cut public spending. This is an unjustified claim as Cameron outlined his vision for society years before the financial crash. Cameron had other

14 David Cameron, Victory Speech, 6th December 2005.

policies to show that the Conservatives in government could be progressive. His commitment to spending 0.7% of GDP on International Aid (more than almost any country in the world) meant that between 2010–16, the aid budget nearly doubled. This was at a time of spending cuts in nearly every other department.

As a final point, Cameron's most significant social reform is the introduction of same-sex marriage. This was forced through to show that the Conservative Party had changed beyond recognition and that they had atoned for the sin of Section 28.

The 2015 General Election was another positive step forward in Cameron's attempt at changing the Party so that the MPs reflected the country it sought to represent. At least this is the case when it came to more women and ethnic minorities being elected. Sixty-eight women were elected in 2015 which was over 20% of the Conservative Parliamentary Party. This was another 40% increase in women MPs and showed encouraging progress. It was also a successful movement towards a more diverse Parliamentary Party and female Conservative MPs showed that they could achieve this on merit and did not need a patronising idea like an all-women's shortlist.

One third of Cameron's cabinet after the 2015 election comprised of women, which showed another great stride forward. The Conservatives progress on ethnic minorities was also noteworthy as 17 BME candidates were elected in 2015. This was over 5% of the Party but what was most pleasing was the fact that 33% of minorities voted Conservative. This had more than doubled since 2010 and the Conservatives had clearly improved the image of the Party to make it more attractive to minorities.

Conservatives from private schooled backgrounds dropped from 54% to 48% after the 2015 General Election. While this is a welcome trend, this was still a far higher proportion than any other party in parliament. Four out of the five people writing the 2015 Tory Manifesto went to Eton which did not help the public's view of the Conservatives. Indeed, after the election over half of the cabinet had attended a fee paying school. Michael Gove, a close confidante to Cameron stated in 2014 that no other developed country had such a 'bastion of privilege' and attacked the 'preposterous' amount of old Etonions in the Conservative inner circle.[15] In the following chapters I wish to outline Conservative policies which will improve social mobility in Britain and at the same time help us lose the image of elitism and privilege.

Implications of Cameron's Leadership

Under David Cameron's leadership of the Conservatives between 2005–16, decontaminating the public's view of the Party was always at the forefront of his mind. There was a presumption that many activists who disagreed with the leadership over policy had nowhere to go and the Conservative Coalition would remain. Entering into government with the Liberal Democrats assured a move to the centre ground, especially on social and cultural issues.

The Tory modernisers failure to support an EU Referendum and the failure to get immigration numbers down alienated many on the Conservative Right. This resulted in Nigel Farage's UKIP becoming increasingly more attractive. The Coalition Government increased International Aid at a time when public services were being cut and introduced same-sex marriage when it wasn't in the Party's manifesto. This led to UKIP attracting Conservative voters. In 2013, it was claimed a member of the Conservative leadership called the grassroots membership, 'swivel-eyed loons'; this merely confirmed what many activists thought the leadership believed about them.

15 https://www.theguardian.com/politics/2014/mar/15/michael-gove-old-etonians-conservative-david-cameron [Accessed 19th February 2017]

Even with a promise of an EU Referendum in 2013, this did not stop Douglas Carswell and Mark Reckless defecting to UKIP in 2014. Although many Ukippers returned to the Conservatives for the 2015 General Election, just as many stayed with UKIP as some felt the Tories had changed beyond recognition.

The modernisation of the Conservatives had more of a success with centre ground voters than those on the centre Right. This did not appear to be the case for most of the parliament as many centre ground voters became disaffected with the Conservatives austerity policies and the perception that the poorest were suffering at the benefit of the rich. Many centrist voters supported welfare reform but when it looked like welfare cuts were taking priority over reform this made many feel uncomfortable. The removal of the Spare Room Subsidy (or the Bedroom Tax to critics) being the most poignant example of this.

Public services like the NHS and schools were under financial pressure throughout these years. The public sector pay cap and cuts to local government meant that many centrist voters stopped voting Conservative. Lack of investment in housing meant that many of those who were aspirational and not particularly political, 'couldn't get on in life'. Nonetheless, by the end of the parliament many of the tough decisions taken by the government kept many of the centrists onside.

In the 2015 General Election, the Conservatives gained 27 seats as centrist voters flocked from the Liberal Democrats to Tory, although this was certainly not because of love for the Tories. Voters did not trust Labour with the economy, did not believe Ed Miliband would be a competent prime minister and most certainly did not wish to see him propped up by the SNP. Despite voters thinking the party was 'elitist' and 'out of touch', the doubts about Ed Miliband led to many voting Conservative, as they still trusted the Party in terms of economic credibility and strong leadership.

Theresa May Government 2016–Present

Theresa May's speech upon entering Downing Street filled me with an abundance of optimism as she was speaking the aspirational language of many people in Britain. I hoped in the following years she would develop a vision for the country that showed the Tories were on the side of ordinary people. To me this meant there should be no 'no-go areas' for the Conservatives. This meant a full frontal charm offensive to the working-class North of England, Scotland, to ethnic minorities, to students and to public sector workers. I felt Cameron made some progress on this but a genuine one nation Conservative Party can only be a reality if we can reach out to all of the country.

May made a strong start in promoting a meritocratic cabinet as 70% of her ministers had attended a state school. This cabinet boasted the highest proportion of state schooled MPs since Clement Attlee's Government of 1945. After the turbulence of Brexit, May was seen as a safe pair of hands to steward the nation through troubled waters. Opinion polls showed that many UKIP and Labour voters were attracted to a May-led Conservative Party, with the Party reaching around 50% in some opinion polls.

With the Conservatives consistently ahead by around 20% of a seemingly hapless Labour Party in the opinion polls, on the 18th April 2017, May announced a snap general election. This was seen as risky by some but most pointed to the popularity of May since she became prime minister. May desired to increase her majority from 17 to a landslide victory. What followed was one of the most shocking campaigns in British political history which has led to the Conservatives being pigeonholed once again as 'nasty and arrogant'.

The Conservatives were characterised as nasty because the manifesto proposed removing free school meals from primary school children. Changes to social care were dubbed in the media as a 'dementia tax', and removing the winter fuel allowance from pensioners without specifying a cut off threshold alienated core voters. These proposals completely overshadowed good policies proposed on shareholder's power over pay and extra money for the NHS.

The Conservative Party also came across as arrogant. Theresa May should have absolutely torn Jeremy Corbyn apart over his past sympathy with terrorist organisations, his nonsensical economics and highlighted the fact that his policies didn't add up. Many reasonable swing voters expressed to me that refusing to debate him made the Conservatives look arrogant. Instead of meeting real people, there were too many stage-managed events which made the Conservatives look out of touch. We should have remembered how effective John Major was on his soap box when he campaigned in 1992.

When the exit poll was shown at 10pm, it showed the Conservatives as the largest party but short of an overall majority. The collapse of UKIP meant the Conservatives increased their share of the vote from 37% to 42% but with Labour increasing theirs from 30% to 40%, the result was a hung parliament.

What has the 2017 General Election meant for increasing the diversity of the Parliamentary Party? Sixty-seven women were elected to parliament which was one down on 2015 but still remained over 20% of the Conservative Parliamentary Party. This showed a stalling in recent progress but this isn't surprising as the Conservatives lost 13 seats. The amount of ethnic minority candidates elected proved to be a more positive story as this increased from 17 to 19 MPs. Although regrettably it looks like the Conservatives took a backward step on the ethnic minority vote as many may have been susceptible to the scaremongering around Brexit.

Some 45% of current Conservative MPs went to a fee paying school which is less than 2015 but still a far larger amount than any other party in parliament. Even with this amount of Tory MPs being from private schools, polls show more working-class people voted Conservative than ever before. In parallel to this more middle-class people voted Labour than ever before which led to a dramatic increase in their share of the vote. This has been underreported by the media and gives the Conservatives a solid foundation going forward with working-class voters.

Another underrepresented group voted in their largest number for many years. Only 43% of young people voted in 2015 but some estimates show that up to 70% voted in 2017. Unfortunately, they overwhelmingly voted for Labour and the result showed that the Conservatives face an existential crisis in winning a majority again particularly if more young people are voting than ever before. This is fantastic for democracy but as I hope to illustrate in this book, we need a positive vision for attracting more young people to vote Conservative.

The electorate left the Conservatives no choice but to enter into a pact with the Democratic Unionist Party (DUP) of Northern Ireland. Many reasonable centre ground liberal voters who we should be attracting do not like this pact. The DUP certainly shares the Conservatives views on strong defence, security and some economic policies, but we are very far away on others. Social issues are where we differ profoundly due their questionable views on gay and women's rights.

The DUP have not requested any changes to legislation regarding women's and gay rights but as Conservatives we need to stand up for our recent track record on these issues, reminding the public they have very different social views to our own. The leader of the Scottish Conservatives, Ruth Davidson, is a working-class lesbian who showed that when the Tories connect with ordinary people we can be successful. As well as a gay leader in Scotland, it is the Conservatives who introduced same-sex marriage and between 2010–15 had more gay MPs than all other political parties put together. We need to be sure that the pact with the DUP stays focused on confidence and supply, and ensure they do not influence our social policy, as the label of the ‘nasty party’ will be embedded further.

Moving Forward: Reinvigorating the Conservatives by Creating a True 'House of Commons'

Throughout this book I aim to portray a vision, with policy answers to improve the Conservative cause in Britain. I genuinely believe it is the Conservative Party who has the best chance of making Britain a more meritocratic society. There are many weaknesses to the Conservatives reputation with the public, but fundamentally we are the best Party to improve the life chances of ordinary people. Crucially, this is because we are the Party of aspiration.

When John Prescott spoke out after the 2015 General Election crying "What the 'eck does aspiration mean?" it spoke volumes of the modern Labour Party. The public still know that with all our faults as a party it is us who care about improving home ownership (as Thatcher's legacy shows). We are the Party who are seen to be strong leaders and are able to make the most difficult decisions. We are seen as competent and able to be trusted with the taxpayer's money.

As the Conservatives experienced with Black Wednesday and the Labour Party experienced with the financial crash, economic credibility is crucial when the public make up their mind at an election. On societal issues the general public know that it is the Conservatives that will protect family values and encourage British citizens to know their responsibilities as well as their rights. When it comes to law and order the public know that a moderate Conservative Party will protect the interests of the victim much more than the bleeding heart liberals who care more about the perpetrator of the crime.

I have not written this chapter to preach to the converted about the strengths of the Conservative Party, I have written it to mainly identify our weaknesses. It is only when we identify weaknesses within our brand, we can develop the vision and policies to strengthen our voter base. We are not a protest party like Corbyn's Labour, who do not wish to recognise their weaknesses and only preach to those who already support their cause. The Conservative Party are still identified as 'out of touch' and 'elitist' by many parts of the electorate. Paradoxically, even though we are seen as the party of aspiration, we are still seen to be the party of entrenched privilege. Many of the previously mentioned public relations disasters and policy decisions has not helped improve this perception.

If we are to strengthen our voter base and reach out to all parts of the electorate we need to tackle this concern. In the following chapters I seek to outline policy proposals, many of which will encourage people to feel more comfortable to vote for Conservative. In parallel to broadening our appeal, we need to widen our membership base with innovative initiatives and reformed party structures.

The current Conservative Party is a diverse group of professionals ranging from former postmen, to nurses, to charity workers, to doctors and many more fantastic representatives. But there is still a long way to go to make the Conservative Parliamentary Party more representative of the country as a whole. Although the Conservatives truly believe that 'it is not about where you are from but where you are going', the public will not believe this statement if they see MPs that have all attended the same school, university or come from the same profession.

Although we need to broaden our base, I am resolutely against so called 'positive discrimination' to make this happen as no discrimination is positive. Labour's top down all women's shortlists, which have been constant throughout the last 20 years, have yet to result in a female leader. They claim to be the party of equality but yet it is the Conservatives who have had two female prime ministers, without the introduction of all women's shortlists.

There needs to be a concerted effort to get many more ordinary people into frontline politics based on meritocracy. If the image of the Conservatives is to change in order to look more meritocratic we need to open up the Party. Open primaries are one way of doing this. This is where the local electorate choose the candidate beyond the franchise of the membership and has led to strong independent voices like Sarah Wollaston being elected. This sort of system can lead to more open debate and the political parties being in touch with the local electorate. In addition to this, the Campaign for Conservative Democracy has written about providing candidate bursaries, or even loans to widen the field of people who wish to stand for parliament.

Conservative Party structures should be democratised to make it more open to new members. During William Hague's spell as leader he adopted the 'Blueprint for Change' document in the bid to democratise the party structures. This gave members a vote when choosing the leader and opportunities to vote on party policies. Regrettably this direction of travel did not continue in the subsequent years and the Conservatives are now seen by academics and commentators as the most top-down and least democratic of the main political parties.

If the Conservatives are to be sustained as a grassroots campaigning organisation we need to attract new members. We need reforming and forward thinking initiatives from within the Party to allow members to have more of an input on policy. This means promoting and extending the Conservative Policy Forum and make members aware that they can join when they sign up to the Party. There should be a policy discussion forum to debate a local or national issue each month in each constituency up and down the country. At the time of writing this, the Conservative Policy Forum has 400 Facebook likes. This figure should be at least 40,000 likes and this would be achievable if such forums were perceived to have a real influence over policy.

The Primrose League was a broad-based mass membership organisation which peaked in the early twentieth century. It aimed to spread Conservative messages of fighting for Queen and Country and promoting free enterprise. In 1910, there were nearly 2 million members at a time when there was an electorate of only 7.7 million. Fast forward 41 years and there was nearly 3 million members of the Conservative Party. In recent years the membership of the Conservative Party has dwindled to roughly 100,000 people. We face an existential crisis as a party if we do not start attracting more members.

I will be brutally honest in my criticism of Corbyn's Labour Party throughout this book but he must be praised for his ability to increase the Labour Party's membership to over half a million. The Conservatives will always find it difficult to build such an enormous movement as we are the party of making tough decisions in government, not standing on a street corner in perpetual protest. Nevertheless, we shouldn't be scared of building a mass movement with true democratic discussion, debate and policy input.

With over half the Conservative Party's membership being over 60, we need to think about the next 20 years and who will be knocking on the electorate's doors to spread our message. We should utilise the modern ways of communicating with voters through the sophisticated databases that each party has and through this we can turn the voter into a member. The Conservatives use social media and advertising to target voters at election time, however this tool should be consistently used to attract new members.

In relation to advertising, Robert Halfon has proposed a visual change that the Conservatives should enact. He propositions that we change the Party logo by swapping the tree for a ladder. Having a tree as our Party logo means little to the Conservative members but a ladder symbols aspiration and opportunity, the very definition of our beliefs.

More traditional methods of attracting members should also be used by the Party. As I've stated, policy discussion could help with this, so could public meetings called by the local MP to discuss local and national issues. These meetings could lead to more local people joining the party (especially if the MP has a popular following). Furthermore, offering a first year discount membership or a free one-day pass to the party conference might spark the interest of voters. If members believe they have a genuine say in the Party (both locally and nationally) then an increase of numbers and engagement would naturally follow.

From 42% to 50%

Margaret Thatcher famously said "Standing in the middle of the road is very dangerous; you get knocked down by the traffic from both sides". In many ways I understand why David Cameron sought to move the Conservatives back to the centre ground. In 2005, after eight years of Labour rule and a seemingly irrelevant Conservative Party, a change of direction was needed.

In a bid to attract more centrist voters, the Conservatives prioritised global warming, restorative justice, gay rights and a commitment to the same public spending as the Labour Government. The Party moved to the Right in government but still allowed mass immigration, doubled International Aid and was only reluctantly persuaded on an EU referendum. This however created a vacuum for a party like UKIP to thrive. Many of the Conservatives core voters believed in more emphasis on tax cuts, patriotism and family values. It is clear much of the core vote felt neglected throughout this period.

The EU referendum, with the promise of more control over immigration and our own laws and trade, meant many disillusioned Tories have now returned from UKIP. But the 2017 General Election showed we cannot rely on UKIP members returning to the Conservatives to give us a majority government. Evidence shows about 50% of UKIP supporters at the 2015 election moved to the Tories in 2017. This was enough to increase our share of the vote from 37% to 42%

but with the Labour Party keeping much of their working-class base and attracting record amounts of middle-class voters, it did not prove to be enough.

However, it is telling that some of the Labour working-class supporters have transferred allegiance to the Conservatives. The working-class Brexit supporters of the Labour Party are now being sneered at by the metropolitan Labour leadership and are increasingly considering the Conservatives as an option. Jeremy Corbyn's lack of patriotism, sympathy with terrorists and his belief in unlimited welfare has further alienated him from Labour's working-class base. Ideas proposed by Theresa May including workers on company boards and a firmer approach to immigration and crime has clearly convinced some to vote Conservative. Even more would have voted Conservative if it wasn't for the 2017 manifesto being so toxic. With policy proposals such as the means testing of free school meals and the winter fuel allowance, we managed to alienate many natural Conservatives.

It is obvious that in the last couple of years the Conservatives have not spoken to Remain voters, people worried about perpetual austerity and those who worry about their children's life chances. With current levels of Labour support, the Conservatives may need to win 50% of the vote in a general election to win a majority government.

As well as reinvigorating the membership, we need attractive policies which can appeal to millions of new voters. Attracting more working-class supporters is a fantastic achievement but as we are losing more young voters than ever before, we need to show how capitalism and a Tory government can serve their interests. As a party, we need to stop playing it safe and propose a radical manifesto. That means debating with our opponents. That means answering questions, not reeling off bland vacuous slogans. That means getting out there and meeting real people.

Setting out an inspiring vision, coupled with a true focus on the 'just about managing' will help attract many more voters back to the Conservatives. We need to introduce policies which will empower young people to buy a home at a time when they think it is impossible. We need to show that welfare reform is more important than welfare cuts by making Universal Credit more generous. We need to give shareholders the power to veto executive pay-outs when undeserved; this could go a long way to take on the crony capitalists. We need to tackle student worries about debt whilst still arguing a case for a financial contribution.

During the course of this book I will write about many of my own ideas to build an economy to work for everyone and to promote social mobility. Such ideas I hope will be adopted into policy in the coming years. I believe that the ideas proposed in this book will improve the image of the Conservative Party both in perception as well as in reality.

2 Economy

"Let us never forget this fundamental truth: The State has no source of money other than money which is earned. If the State wishes to spend more it can do so only by borrowing or taxing you more. It is not good thinking someone else will pay – that 'someone else' is you. There is no such thing as public money; there is only taxpayers' money."[16] *– Margaret Thatcher, 1983*

Introduction

Every Conservative understands that social mobility is not possible without a strong economy. The Left often tut, groan and shout down this statement. Admittedly an emphasis on a strong economy can come across as dry to most of the electorate. Nonetheless if we are going to have well-funded hospitals, pensions and schools; we can only achieve this if we have an economy where confidence is high amongst consumers and businesses are flourishing. As a consequence of this, employment will be high which means tax revenues are being increased to fund our cherished public services.

Conservatives understand that the redistribution of wealth comes through tax cuts in a growing economy, not crushing enterprise through punitive tax rates. Labour tirade about

16 Margaret Thatcher, Conservative Party Conference, 14th October 1983.

constantly spending more money on absolutely everything, but those who talk about the redistribution of wealth need to remember wealth needs to be created in the first place through a thriving private sector.

Although I masqueraded as a socialist for a year or two, this was never going to be sustained as I was brought up by a fiscally conservative mother who had a great influence on my beliefs when it came to sound economic management. I was raised for most of my childhood in a single-parent family, my mother worked in retail and then as a receptionist and in secretarial positions. Raising three children on one modest income taught me great conservative values like hard work, living within your means and self-reliance. It amazes me when people ask how I'm a Conservative with my background. I often reply with, with my background, how could I not have turned out to be a Conservative?

In 2010, with the Coalition Government entering into power with the largest budget deficit of any major economy and the largest of any British Government since World War Two, promoting a more meritocratic and equal country was always going to be a monumental task. I will provide a critical analysis of the inheritance left by Labour in 2010 and how the Coalition and then the Conservative Government managed the economy, particularly under George Osborne's stewardship. Osborne was often derided for claiming 'we are all in this together' but was attacked by many from the Left for attempting to 'balance the books on the backs of the poor'. I have a much more nuanced position on this claim and I will illustrate that through his goal of cutting the budget deficit, it can be argued that he did a lot to help people on low and middle incomes.

If you claim to support a truly meritocratic society, where those with talents and ability are able to get to the top; then this means an acceptance of some inequality. As a Conservative I believe in equality of opportunity but certainly not equality of outcome. If we are to promote and improve our society to make it more upwardly mobile, in many areas we need to create a much more level playing field. I accept there is a contradiction in my beliefs on inequality as I believe there to be acceptable and fair inequality and unacceptable and unfair inequality. I will explore this contradiction further later on in this chapter.

Linked to the pertinent issue of inequality and social mobility is the need to improve capitalism itself. I believe capitalism needs to be improved because I fear what will happen if left unreformed. The Left should not have a monopoly on challenging crony capitalism and tax avoidance/evasion. Capitalism has lifted hundreds of millions of people out of poverty in the last several decades and our livelihoods depend on it. However, it is clear that the impact of globalisation has hit some our poorest communities the hardest in the last decade. If we are to build a more socially just post-Brexit society, we need to ensure that Margaret Thatcher's 'popular capitalism' can prevail once more.

1997–2010: Record of the Last Labour Government

When Labour steamrollered into office with the great landslide of 1997, they could not have asked for a healthier economic inheritance. Resulting from the stewardship of Ken Clarke as Chancellor, the budget deficit was tiny, unemployment was falling and growth was strong. Unfortunately, a strong economy was not enough to keep a very unpopular Conservative Party in government.

Gordon Brown matched the Conservatives tax and spending pledges at the 1997 General Election as the first would-be Labour Government in 18 years aspired to be economically credible with the electorate. After the landslide of 2001, Labour abandoned this idea of controlled public spending and a large spending spree ensued over the next 9 years. In 2000, government spending was 36.8% of GDP.

By 2010, it was 47.1% of GDP. By any measure this is an extraordinary increase in state spending.

George Osborne often attacked Labour for not 'fixing the roof when the sun was shining' – this is unarguably true. After ten years of consistent economic growth (13 years if you include Clarke's Chancellorship), the UK's budget deficit in 2007–08 was over £40 billion. This means the government was borrowing £40 billion more than it was taking in tax, even after 13 years of economic growth. Labour often argue that the Tories falsely claim that they crashed the banks, but no Conservative has ever claimed this. What we do hold against the last Labour Government is that they left Britain woefully unprepared for the crash when it did come.

In April 2015, the Shadow Chief Secretary to the Treasury, Chris Leslie canvassed on my door in Sneinton, Nottingham. I challenged him on Labour's economic record. We had an interesting chat but he did not argue against my point that after ten years of growth there should not have been such a high budget deficit. In the Labour Leadership Election of 2015, Andy Burnham (the Chief Secretary to the Treasury in Gordon Brown's Government) even admitted that Labour spent too much in the run up to the crash.

The belief that a strong growing economy in which the government spends as much money as it takes in, is anathema to Labour. They sit on their moral high horse and are clearly disgusted at the Conservatives economic beliefs. When Liam Byrne left the note in the treasury back in 2010 stating 'sorry there is no money left', he did so as if it was as a joke. If you want to believe in helping the poorest in our society get on in life it is not funny to joke about leaving a budget deficit of over 10% of GDP. This means that when the Coalition Government entered office in 2010, as a nation we were borrowing over £153 billion a year more than we took in tax revenue. Much of this was the fault of greedy bankers and foolish individuals living beyond their means, but the Labour Government was living well beyond its means and they too should take responsibility. Saddling each citizen with thousands of pounds of debt is no way to improve social justice.

The Economy Since 2010: Whose Side Was George Osborne On?

The record of George Osborne as Chancellor is fascinating as he managed to upset all sides of the political spectrum in his pursuit of eradicating the budget deficit. As discussed in the previous chapter, he often managed to alienate the public with the way he presented his Budgets and at first glance he seemed to make some big decisions which had a detrimental impact on the poorest in society.

I will go on to discuss these decisions in further detail throughout this chapter. But if you manage to get past the self-indulgent finger wagging of the *Guardian*, the left-wing protestors and the Twitterazi, there was clearly another side to George Osborne. There was Osborne the progressive, who took more money from the wealthy through many tax rises and ultimately reduced inequality in some key policy areas. After the following evaluation, the reader can make up their own mind.

Let's start with the stereotypical portrayal of George Osborne as the man who sought to balance the budget deficit on the backs of the poor. There is no doubt the 2011 VAT increase disproportionately hit the poorest the hardest and squeezed consumer spending at a time when inflation was rising and wages were stagnating. The public sector pay restraint meant that the wages in the public sector were capped at a time when inflation was much higher. There were significant benefit cuts which were implemented at the behest of Osborne. Most difficult of which was the removal of the spare room subsidy for those claiming Housing Benefit for spare bedrooms. It was quickly dubbed the 'Bedroom Tax' and was seen as an attack on the disabled.

Moreover, was the botched plans of the 2015 Budget to cut the taper rate which would have meant a real terms cut to the poorest people claiming Tax Credits. The other failed welfare reform was the proposed cuts to Personal Independence Payment (PIP) which made Osborne look out of touch and seen to be attacking the vulnerable. Finally, the benefit freeze which included Tax Credits, Child Benefit and Job Seeker's Allowance (JSA), can be seen as a real terms cut when inflation is taken into account.

Conversely, the rise in VAT meant that in real terms the rich would be paying more as higher earners consume more goods and luxuries. To reduce the huge budget deficit, it was clear that VAT, income tax or National Insurance needed to rise. In my view it is always better to tax consumption rather than people's direct incomes. Public sector pay still rose through the salary band system and anybody earning below £21,000 were not subject to the pay limit. This meant the lowest earners in society were not penalised.

The removal of the spare room subsidy was a duplicate of the same policy brought in under Labour for those in the private sector. It was aimed to help encourage those with spare bedrooms to downsize. In the early years of the Coalition, it was shown that even some MPs could claim Tax Credits and it was clear that many middle earners were claiming at the expense of the taxpayer. With the botched Tax Credit and PIP cuts showing Osborne at his weakest, it must be noted that even if these reforms had gone through, we would still have had one of the most generous benefit systems anywhere in the world (people on the Left seem to forget this).

Even with the benefit freeze, welfare spending still rose under the Conservatives throughout every year since entering office. Those who attack Osborne for punishing the poor often cite many of the choices which were made at the top of the income spectrum. The most memorable was the cut of the higher rate of income tax from 50p to 45p. At a time when there was welfare freezes and public sector pay restraint, this was deemed elitist and a 'tax cut for millionaires'.

Regardless of the economics, at a time of austerity this was harmful to the Conservatives' claim that we were 'all in this together'. Cutting corporation tax for big businesses from 28% in 2010 to 19% in 2017 was seen as a tax cut for the richest corporations. Much of the public saw this as a tax cut for those who already did not pay enough in tax in the first place. When Osborne claimed that he had a major success in 2016 by managing to persuade Google to pay £130 million in tax, the public were rightly infuriated. This amounted to Google paying 3% in corporation tax when the rate should have been 20%.

Finally, Osborne was seen to favour the rich by announcing that the inheritance tax threshold would rise to £1 million. This would benefit only the top of society who possess the most wealth. The decisions made by Osborne to cut the higher rate of income tax, corporation tax and inheritance tax gave many on the Left ample opportunity to portray him as elitist and on the side of the rich at the expense of the rest of society.

Contrariwise, the same people seemed to forget that the 45p rate was still higher than under 13 years of Labour rule. It was brought in as a trap for the Tories before the 2010 General Election by Gordon Brown. The cutting of the 50p rate raised more money from the rich as more investors flocked to Britain. Under Osborne, and then Hammond, the top 1% pay over 27% of all income tax. The highest proportion ever. Cutting this tax was a lesson learned from history as when Nigel Lawson cut the higher rate from 83% to 60% he raised more money from the rich as it attracted more business men and women to invest in Britain.

It is the same story with corporation tax. Revenues have increased from cutting corporation tax as having the most competitive tax rate in the G7 has led to more big businesses wishing to invest in Britain. This means more jobs are being created, resulting in more people paying tax, which funds our public services. The raising of the inheritance tax threshold can be seen as acceptable in an era of ridiculously high house prices. It is now perfectly plausible for a £2 million two-bedroom terraced house to be sold in London. Suddenly that inheritance tax threshold slowly rising to £1 million doesn't look like it only benefits the elite after all.

Measures to Help Low Earners

There is a strong argument to suggest that in many ways the Coalition Government and the Conservative Government which followed protected the interests of the lowest paid in society. First and foremost, was the cutting of direct income taxes for over 30 million people and taking the lowest earners out of tax altogether. In 2010, the personal allowance was £6,475. By April 2017 this had been raised to £11,500. This means the allowance has progressively increased well above inflation every year under the Conservatives. By April 2017 this meant anybody who earns over £11,500 will have seen a £1,005 a year tax cut under the Conservatives.

By 2020, the personal allowance will be £12,500 which is another £200 a year taxpayers will be able to keep for themselves. This great achievement has been completely understated throughout the last few years, including by the Conservatives themselves at the 2017 General Election. When I was earning £15,000 a year working in jobs such as a support worker for a homeless hostel, this tax cut was hugely beneficial. It is ridiculous when commentators suggest this tax cut helps middle earners more than lower earners as it proportionately helps lower earners much more.

Research by the Institute of Fiscal Studies have shown that the proportion of working-age adults who do not pay income tax has risen from 34.3% in 2010 to 43.8% by 2016–17.[17]

17 https://www.ifs.org.uk/publications/9178 [Accessed 11th March 2017]

This tax cut for low to middle earners helps people keep more of their own money and has rebalanced the tax system in favour of lower earners.

Other progressive changes introduced under the Conservatives include the National Living Wage. The idea for the minimum wage to be linked to 60% of median earnings is a great policy initiative which shows a commitment to reducing income inequality. In April 2016, the minimum wage went up from £6.70 to £7.20 for over 25s. This was a 6% increase in the wages of the lowest paid and studies show that inequality has been reduced by this measure, as the lowest paid have seen the largest increase in pay. The living wage increased by another 4% in April 2017 which meant that within a year, the lowest earners had seen a £1,500 pay increase. This is an extraordinary achievement from the Conservatives especially as there was what turned out to be unfounded fears that unemployment would rise.

As well as protecting the lowest paid through the increases in the personal allowance and the National Living Wage, the Conservatives have helped children get the best start in life. If we are to build a more meritocratic society, then helping children to develop and reach their full potential during their early years must be a priority. The Coalition brought in free 15 hours a week childcare for the lowest paid parents of two-year-olds. In addition to this, since 2016, parents of three- and four-year-olds have been given access to 30 hours a week free childcare (the equivalent to £5,000 a year paid childcare). This will ensure that the lowest paid working families will be able to give their child the best start in life which in the long run will tackle inequality. This policy has and will support many more mothers re-entering into the work place earlier than might have been expected.

Another way the Conservatives have helped children of the lowest paid is through the Pupil Premium. This is £2.5 billion a year of extra funding provided to schools for children who are on free school meals or are in care. In my current job, in defending the educational interests of children in care, I have seen the Pupil Premium transform the lives of the most disadvantaged. This flexible grant serves many different purposes including extra one-to-one support, smaller class sizes, and widening the cultural opportunities for the child. This is instrumental to reducing inequality and giving the poorest children more of a chance in life. Both free childcare and the Pupil Premium will be discussed further in the chapter on education but it is important to remember that these initiatives were funded when George Osborne was Chancellor.

Tax Rises on High Earners

Looking at the opposite end of the income spectrum, it is completely overlooked that Osborne introduced many tax rises and ended many perks for middle and high earners. The lazy portrayal of him attempting to bring the budget deficit down by attacking low income people does not stand up under scrutiny. In 2010 he faced a Conservative Conference in Birmingham and informed them that over £1 billion a year was given out in Child Benefit to higher rate taxpayers. He duly told the conference that Child Benefit would be taken away from those who earn £44,000 a year. This was a brave move as this would affect many supporters in that conference hall.

In the Emergency Budget of that year, Osborne had already upset many Conservatives when he hiked the rate of capital gains tax (the tax on the profit made when an asset is sold). Under Labour, this was a flat rate of 18% however Osborne raised this for additional rate taxpayers to 28%. This was seen as a progressive move by many but Osborne was accused of stifling investment and entrepreneurship. Without the Liberal Democrats influencing policy, in the 2016 Budget capital gains was cut to 20% for higher rate and 10% for basic rate taxpayers. Labour howled with anger at this decision and it must be said that the optics of this policy was questionable to say the least. Particularly, as at the same time cuts to Personal Independence Payments were being proposed. Nevertheless, the capital gains tax rate for the highest earners would still be higher under the Conservatives than under 13 years of Labour.

Another tax that Osborne raised to collect more money from the wealthy was dividend tax. As this is a tax on shareholders of a company, this was again a difficult issue for the Conservative rank and file to accept. Before the reforms in 2015, the basic rate paid 0%, the higher paid 25% and the additional paid 30.56%. The Budget 2015 brought in a £5,000 personal allowance but rates were hiked (7.5% for basic, 32.5% for higher and 38.1% for additional). According to KPMG, higher rate taxpayers would be up to 25% worse off under the changes brought in by Osborne.[18] This progressive case can be further strengthened with Philip Hammond cutting the dividend allowance from £5,000 to £2,000 at the 2017 Budget.

Contrary to mainstream belief, there was a shift under the Conservatives to reduce inequality when it came to asset wealth and intergenerational fairness. This has mainly taken the form of stamp duty reforms. Under Labour, properties bought over £500,000 were taxed at 4%. This meant somebody who was buying a £500,000 home would be paying exactly the same rate of stamp duty as somebody buying a £10 million home. In 2014, Osborne reformed the whole stamp duty system in a highly progressive way. Osborne replaced the old structure, which meant that if a home fell in a certain band then the entire cost of the home was taxed at that rate. This meant a huge jump in the tax bill when a threshold was crossed.

For instance, a home costing £249,000 meant £2,490 is tax, while one costing £250,001 attracted a bill of over

18 KPMG

£7,500. Osborne removed the cliff edge of each band and ensured the first £125,000 cost of a home would be used as a tax free allowance. On a £180,000 house purchase there would now be no tax on the first £125,000, then there would be a 2% tax on the remaining £55,000. This meant a total bill of £1,100, versus £1,800 before the changes.

As part of the same reforms, anybody buying a house over £937,000 would be worse off. Especially if the home was over £1.5 million as a new 12% rate was brought in. This huge tax rise on stamp duty for the wealthy is now three times higher than under the last Labour Government. If a home was purchased in 2009 for £5 million, £200,000 in stamp duty would have been paid. By 2015, if a home was purchased for the same amount, over £500,000 would have to be paid in stamp duty. This difference of £300,000 on an expensive property showed that the Conservatives took the issue of assets being taxed at the top to reduce inequality very seriously. This huge rise in stamp duty on the wealthiest was further reformed by Osborne when he sought to prevent buy-to-let landlords gaining a further foothold in the market. With many young first time buyers struggling to get on the property ladder, the tax system was used to target those buying second homes.

In the Autumn Statement of 2015, a 3% surcharge in stamp duty was introduced for anybody buying a second home in England and Wales. This meant that for properties worth between £125,000 and £250,000, where the stamp duty was 2%, buy-to-let landlords would now have to pay 5%. For the average buy-to-let purchase of £184,000, an extra £5,520 would be paid in stamp duty. Returning to the aforementioned £5 million home, over £663,000 would now be paid in stamp duty, which is over three times the amount paid under Labour. To add to this tax rise on second home owners, the capital gains cut which was brought in that year did not include them, so they would still be paying the rate of 28% if a higher earner.

Alongside the stamp duty hike, since April 2017 buy-to-let landlords have faced cuts in the amount of tax relief they can claim on mortgage payments. Many in the private rented market claim this will destroy investment, but there is no doubt the use of second homes as income for the wealthy has been scaled back dramatically under the Conservatives.

Tax Avoidance and the Bank Levy

In addition to taxes on individuals, Osborne clearly did more than any other Chancellor in history when it came to clamping down on tax avoidance and taxing the banks. Again, the media portrayal of him as attacking the poor completely overlooks this fact. Before the crash of 2008 tax avoidance had built up steadily by many big businesses and wealthy individuals. In the so called great stability of the 00's public concern was quite low on tax avoidance but when austerity started to bite it soon rocketed up the agenda.

In 2012, the story broke that in 14 years, Starbucks had paid just £8.6 million in corporation tax in the UK. Many from the across the political spectrum were disgusted by this. Other companies like Amazon, Google and McDonald's were also put under the spotlight. The Conservatives undoubtedly saw this as a priority to help close the tax gap and ensure that those at the top could not continue avoiding tax. With estimates of between £34 to £120 billion a year avoided or evaded in tax, this had to be tackled. Osborne closed many tax loopholes in his years as Chancellor and his most notable intervention was the diverted profits tax which was announced in the Budget of 2015. This gave HMRC the powers to tax companies by 25% if they suspected them of structuring their companies to avoid tax.

With corporation tax being significantly lowered to make the UK more attractive, big businesses should be expected more than ever to pay their fair share. In Philip Hammond's first Budget of 2017 he announced that HMRC had raised an extra £140 billion in extra revenue from tax avoidance throughout the last seven years. There is still much to be done but there is no doubt that this government has confronted the major scandal of tax avoidance and evasion head on.

The bank levy was another policy that the Conservatives introduced in the Budget of 2010, to take more tax from the wealthy. This was to ensure that the banks would pay more during the recovery as the crash began with banking. This was a tax on the total size of balance sheets and was mainly paid by the biggest banks. Implementing the bank levy as a joint move with Germany and France, ensured that Britain would keep its competitive edge in Europe whilst asking the richest banks to pay more.

With corporation tax cuts being implemented on a yearly basis under the Conservatives, the bank levy was increased to ensure they did not benefit from this cut. By 2015 it was announced that the bank levy would be gradually decreased but a new 8% surcharge on profits would be introduced instead. This permanent feature of taxing the banks several billion pounds a year more than before has been an important change by the Conservatives, asking those with the broadest shoulders to bare the largest burden. At the same time the taxes implemented have not been so punitive as to scare the large banks to move offshore to other financial centres.

Pensioner Protections

As outlined above, whilst the Conservatives have been in government, they have attempted to tackle intergenerational fairness in housing through making it less attractive for investors to buy second homes. Billions of extra pounds have been taxed in stamp duty and capital gains. Pension reform has been a somewhat different story. In 2010, the Coalition Government brought in the 'triple lock' on pensions. This has meant that pensions have risen each year by the inflation rate, average earnings or 2.5% – whichever is highest. It is important to note why this policy was implemented.

In 2001, the average pensioner was £70 a week worse off than their fellow citizen who was in work (after housing costs). Following six years of the triple lock (and low wages for working households) according to the Resolution Foundation[19] the typical pensioner is now £20 a week better off than the typical working age earner. This is a huge step forward in how we treat our elderly but it is also a very costly one. Most budgets have been cut since 2010 but pension spending has increased by 25%.

Osborne believed that the spiralling costs of pensions had to be restrained as he attempted to cut the budget deficit. He refused to cut the winter fuel allowance, TV licence and the free bus pass from the better off pensioners but he did consider changing the pension tax relief system. Under the current system, pension savers receive tax relief at the same rate as their income tax – meaning basic rate taxpayers receive relief at 20% and higher rate taxpayers at 40% and 45%. The proposal to introduce arrangements similar to an ISA, with no tax relief on contributions but withdrawals free from tax, would have given a significant short-term boost to the government at the expense of lower tax revenue later.

An alternative option considered by the Treasury was for flat rate relief, which would have benefited basic rate taxpayers and cut reliefs for higher earners. Before the 2016 Budget the government decided not to go along with this policy even though it would have raised billions in revenue. I suspect this was mainly due to the upcoming EU Referendum and the government did not wish to upset older voters as they were most likely to vote.

With a 20-point opinion poll lead during the 2017 General Election, the Conservative Manifesto proposed to introduce 'intergenerational fairness' by reforming several pensioner

19 http://www.resolutionfoundation.org/media/press-releases/recent-retirees-drive-pensioner-incomes-above-those-of-working-families/ [Accessed 11th March 2017]

benefits. First, the triple lock on pensions would become a double lock. This meant that pensions would increase by the highest between either inflation or wages, but not the arbitrary 2.5%. Reducing the triple lock to a double lock was seen by many as fair but with Labour promising to keep the triple lock, this went down badly with core Conservatives and older voters in general. With inflation or wages usually above 2.5% this would have saved little money anyway. Second, the winter fuel allowance was to be means tested. Again, many saw this as fair but as the manifesto gave no indication of the cut-off point, this left many pensioners worried. Finally, the social care reform proposed that people should be expected to pay for their own social care, out of their own assets. This was quickly labelled as a 'dementia tax'. Whatever the merits of these policies, some MPs reported them going down as a 'bucket of cold sick' on the doorstep. All proposed policies have now been scrapped since the election resulted in a hung parliament.

Employment Since 2010: Britain's Jobs Boom

Working as an employability adviser for a charity in Nottingham throughout 2015, I saw first-hand the positives and negatives of employment in modern Britain. Part of my role involved working in several job centres in Nottingham and I will document my experiences later in this chapter. During my time in one of the job centres, I was struck when I was given the overall figures of how unemployment had fallen in the job centres since 2010. Being informed there was a drop in cases in one job centre from 2000 to 400 job seekers between 2010 and 2015 is a remarkable achievement and one which has been seen throughout all regions of our country.

The fantastic achievement of the overall employment and unemployment figures since the Conservatives came into power has been grossly underreported in the media. In May 2010, unemployment had risen above 2.5 million with a rate of 8%. After seven years of Conservative Government in September 2017 the unemployment rate was 4.3%, standing at less than 1.5 million. This is the lowest figure since the summer of 1975.

In the same period, youth unemployment dropped from over 18% to just under 11%. More than 2.5 million apprenticeships have been created since 2010 which has given many young people an alternative to attending school until the age of 18. When the Conservatives unveiled the Emergency Budget in 2010, the Labour Party claimed that the government's austerity would result in increasing unemployment to 3 million people. Coming from a party that have consistently left unemployment higher when leaving office than when they came into power, this was incredibly cheeky. This false claim never came to pass and in actual fact it was quite the reverse. Instead, what we achieved was the highest rate of employment on record. Contrary to people's fears, unemployment has continued to drop in the year after the EU Referendum. But how has this happened? And what sorts of jobs have been created under the Conservatives?

A huge part of the Conservatives appeal in the last decade has been an emphasis on the idea that the best route out of poverty is a job. The best way to promote social mobility and have a strong family is through having a job. This rhetoric has truly been turned into reality across the whole of our nation. Each region in the United Kingdom has seen strong employment growth and so have many groups in society who have historically had low participation rates in the workforce.

Since 2010, under the Conservatives we have seen more women in work than ever before. This includes both women with children and also single parents. In particular, free childcare for many has helped in attracting more women than ever into the labour market. There is a record amount of people from ethnic minorities in work which is another fantastic record but there is still an employment gap between them and the rest of society, which means there is still much more to be done to continue this trend. Pensioners are working longer as many see the value of continuing to work and keep active. This employment rate has doubled in recent years and perks like not paying National Insurance make it attractive and worthwhile for many pensioners to continue to work. Finally, there are more disabled people in work than ever before. This is partly as a result of welfare reforms, which encourage those who can work to work and incentives are being offered to businesses to take on those with disabilities.

Over the last seven years, helping all of the previously mentioned groups into work has meant that there are now fewer workless households than we've ever seen before. This is a great achievement but as I will discuss later in this chapter, there is much more to be done. Regrettably, it cannot be said that that there are more young people in work than ever before. Back in 2010, 18% of 16–24 year olds were out of work. Thankfully there has been a substantial fall since then. This drop has taken place for several different reasons including over 2.5 million more apprenticeships being available since 2010 and National Insurance contributions have been cut for employers taking on young people.

The gap in the mandatory minimum wage means many employers would opt to employ a young person instead of a more experienced counterpart. Welfare reforms have incentivised more young people into work as Job Seekers and Housing Benefit conditions have become more stringent. August 2017's youth unemployment figures show that excluding those in full-time education, 10.6% of young people remain unemployed. This is still too high in my opinion as it is more than double the general unemployment rate. Initiatives to tackle this problem will be further outlined later in this chapter.

On the bright side, relatively speaking our youth unemployment has been extremely low compared to the

Eurozone countries. Greek and Spanish youth unemployment reached 60% at its peak and remained at 44% for both countries by 2016. Other Eurozone countries like France, Italy and Portugal have similarly high youth unemployment which has led to many of their citizens flocking to Britain to find work in recent years. It is an astonishing feat that between the years 2010 and 2015 the United Kingdom has seen a larger increase in employment than the rest of the European Union put together.

Explanations for the Jobs Boom

How has employment increased so dramatically since the Conservatives came into government back in 2010? I believe there are three major reasons for this. First, business incentives were put in place by the Conservatives to attract big businesses and higher earners to invest in the UK. This in turn has led to 3 million more private sector jobs being created in the last seven years which means 3 million people with a pay-packet every month partially due to competitive tax rates. As previously mentioned, corporation tax was cut from 28% in 2010 to 19% by 2017. This means we have the most competitive tax rate out of all major industrialised countries which has resulted in a private sector jobs boom in recent years. In addition to this, more revenue has been collected in corporation tax because of this competitive tax rate. In 2009–10 corporation tax raised £36 billion in revenue at a rate of 28%. By 2016–17 over £50 billion was raised with a lower rate of 20%.

These figures are self-explanatory and this is why I am incredulous when I hear that the Labour Party are planning to abolish tuition fees at a cost of £11 billion a year with a 7% rise in corporation tax. This is the very definition of 'fake maths'. As well as big businesses being incentivised to invest in Britain, the evidence shows that cutting the top rate of tax from 50p to 45p has encouraged many individuals who run medium to large businesses to invest in Britain. In 2010, 24.4% of all income tax was raised by the higher earners, this rose to 27.5% by 2016. Having an additional rate of less than 50% means investors see Britain as a refuge from higher income tax rates. This included France where the 75% tax rate implemented by President Hollande meant that many rich people simply fled the country and took their money with them.

The second reason for this jobs boom and low unemployment has been the tax, minimum wage and welfare changes under the Conservatives. Put simply the government have made it much more attractive to be in work rather than be on welfare. As already stated cutting income tax by raising the tax free personal allowance has meant that many lower wage families have been able to keep more of their hard-earned money in the first place. Alongside people being able to keep more of their own money, the 10% rise in the minimum wage within a year has meant that wages are significantly increasing for the lowest paid.

When the Conservatives entered government in May 2010 the minimum wage was £5.80 an hour and the tax free personal allowance was £6,475. By April 2017 the minimum wage had increased to £7.50 for over 25s and the personal allowance had increased to £11,500. This means that the average 25-year-old on the minimum wage would be better off by £290 a month after tax within that period. This has been a significant achievement in the goal of striving to create a high wage, low income tax society.

Under Labour, wages were kept low and taxes high as welfare subsidised many people to not work or work less hours. Benefit freezes and the overall benefit cap have encouraged many people to seek a job. I found this during my time working with unemployed people and helping them get into work. In late 2016 the Office for National Statistics (ONS) released figures showing the number of children in

UK households where no adult was in work had fallen to its lowest level since records began two decades ago.[20] The government's overall welfare changes will be scrutinised further later on in this book.

The third major reason for the rise of employment since 2010 has been the explosion in self-employed workers. The general narrative from the media is that self-employment has largely been driven by the so called 'gig economy', where people are working in low wage jobs with no benefits or work entitlements. Clearly, there are many issues arising from the gig economy which need to be debated and discussed however research shows that the rapid growth in self-employment has been driven by people in higher paid jobs, not the lower end. The Resolution Foundation has found that 57% of the growth in self employment since 2009 has been amongst educated people working in law, accountancy, health services and management consultancy.[21] They are generally earning £45,000 to £65,000 a year. The fastest growth of self-employment since 2009 has been in advertising, public administration and banking, but self-employment among taxi drivers has only risen 7% in that time. Many enjoy the flexibility of self-employment and the chance to 'be your own boss'. On the other hand, paid maternity leave and holiday entitlements are forfeited by this self-employment.

The government have sought to support many job seekers to find self-employment by the creation of the New Enterprise Allowance. After submitting an idea, a business mentor helps in the development and advises throughout. A weekly allowance is provided for up to 26 weeks and a loan is given for start-up costs. This support by government to create the self-employed of the future has led to thousands

20 Office for National Statistics, Working and workless households in the UK: April to June 2016.

21 http://www.resolutionfoundation.org/publications/a-tough-gig-the-nature-of-self-employment-in-21st-century-britain-and-policy-implications/ [Accessed 11th March 2017]

of new businesses being created through the New Enterprise Allowance.

Britain's jobs boom has undoubtedly been a major success since 2010 but the rise of the gig economy has been a challenging side effect for the government to deal with. As well as the positive stories of self-employment throughout the last seven years there has been a surge in bogus self-employment. It is estimated that out of the 5 million self-employed workers in the UK, about 500,000 (10%) are in bogus self-employment.[22] This includes companies like Uber who have complete control of their drivers but seek to classify their workers as self-employed. This means that workers miss out on holiday pay, the government miss out on tax revenues as less National Insurance is paid and responsible businesses could be undercut. These sorts of unscrupulous business practices have been on the rise in recent years.

Additionally, zero-hour contracts have received substantial media coverage over the last few years. This is when the employer is not obliged to provide any minimum working hours, while the worker is not obliged to accept any work offered. There are of course terrible stories of people having to report in at 7 am and be told there was no work for that day or stories of Sports Direct using these contracts in a punitive manner. Overall, I must confess that I find the hyperbole around zero-hour contracts ridiculous. Figures from September 2016 show that 903,000 people in the UK were on zero-hour contracts, this is only 2.9% of the workforce. Many of the workers on these contracts are students and this flexible working arrangement suits them perfectly fine. I am an example of this as during my five years on a zero-hour contract working at McDonald's, I had the flexibility to take weeks off work to study for exams or go on holiday.

22 http://www.telegraph.co.uk/finance/personalfinance/11810003/500000-self-employed-workers-cheated-out-of-holiday-pay-sick-leave-and-pensions.html [Accessed 11th March 2017]

When Ed Miliband piously pontificated at the 2015 General Election that he would end the 'epidemic of zero-hours contracts', he embarrassed himself (not for the first time). Corbyn has continued with this Labour policy of banning zero-hour contracts and if he had won the 2017 election this would have cost jobs for those who sought flexible working arrangements.

An Economy that Worked for Everyone?

What has been the Conservatives record so far on creating an economy that promotes social mobility and tackles unjust inequalities? The overarching economic mission of the Conservatives has been to create a lower income tax, higher wage and lower welfare economy. Whilst at the same time, they had the predominant task of reducing the budget deficit to sustainable levels. Growth slowed when the Conservatives first took power but the government recovered and Britain became the fastest growing economy in the G20 by 2014.

What was interesting about the slogan 'long-term economic plan' is that it had an authentic ring to it. The long-term economic plan led to the creation of 3 million jobs resulting in more people in work than ever before, over 2.5 million apprenticeships, the introduction of the living wage, the reduction of income tax by £1,000 per year and 600,000 less worklessness households. There is no greater help for social mobility in the economy than by cutting lower earners taxes, raising their wages and reforming welfare so it pays to work. But I must concede that tough decisions have undoubtedly been made since 2010 and I have been openly critical where I feel it is justified.

All of the above achievements were managed at the same time as the deficit being cut by three-quarters between 2010–17. The terrible inheritance that the Coalition faced in 2010 cannot be overstated. We had the highest budget deficit of all major economies and swift action needed to be taken to cut the deficit. This had to be prioritised above everything else and all aspects of society felt the pain. Whether it was people on the lowest incomes with benefit freezes and VAT increases; the middle-class Child Benefit removal and stamp duty hikes; or the wealthiest with huge hikes in dividends tax and the clamping down on tax avoidance.

I am a firm believer that austerity was a necessity as, if we had not managed to take control of our public spending, our public spending would have inevitably taken control of us. The experiences of Eurozone countries like Greece are a pertinent reminder of this hard truth, however the General Election of 2017 has signalled the death of austerity. Going into the election promising more austerity for another five years was a difficult sell and there was certainly a case for a modest increase in public spending as the deficit had been reduced by three-quarters. To help renew our economic policies, I will detail some areas where public spending should increase and taxes on the lowest earners should be reduced. Conservatives also need to think of further ways to tax wealth without attacking wealth creation.

Moving Forward: The Conservative Party and Inequality

Many Conservatives are generally coy about discussions on inequality as we don't want to be seen as attacking the rich, those who are aspirational and ultimately deterring the most talented from coming to Britain in the first place. We often point to the fact that equality of living standards is much more important than equality of income. Throughout my time employed as a support worker in a homeless hostel or when I worked in an alternative education provision, I noticed that many of the most disadvantaged people in society had a smartphone and access to the internet. The fact that anybody in Britain with access to the internet has more information at their fingertips than any British prime minister or American president did 20 years ago is extraordinary.

Although reducing the gap in inequality of living standards is more important than inequality of income, there are serious issues of inequality in our society. The public have been rightly outraged with many big businesses who have not paid their fair share of tax. Small businesses feel that they are undercut by larger businesses who act like monopolies in a rigged market. Many young people are dismayed because they can't afford their first home because of absurdly high house prices. I will propose radical Tory policies to reduce inequality, promote social mobility and further rebalance the tax system which does not mean an enlarged welfare state. At the same time, we always need to remember that a truly free market and a competitive thriving economy is crucial to promoting this agenda.

Those who talk about redistribution of wealth need to remember wealth needs to be created in the first place. Labour believes that the way to address inequality is through drawing more people into welfare dependency, both with in-work and out of work benefits. I have a diametrically opposed point of view. We need to continue the move towards a higher wage, lower tax and lower welfare country. Meritocracy is a far more attractive vision for the country than equality of outcome. If everybody gets the same amount of income no matter what their input into society, then what's the point of getting out of bed in the morning?

A reasonable amount of inequality will always be needed, especially in a truly meritocratic society. Big questions need to be raised on 'fair' and 'unfair' inequality. Is it fair for a drug addict on benefits living in a homeless hostel to be paid more money in benefits than the cleaner who picks up their heroin needles each morning? On the other end of the spectrum is it fair that big companies can divert their profits through tax loopholes and therefore pay a lower rate of tax than that cleaner working in the homeless hostel?

In terms of assets, is it fair that two loving parents who worked hard on modest incomes, saving for their child's future, will face 40% inheritance tax because of conflated house prices? I don't pretend to have all the answers, I am just pointing out that there is 'fair' and 'unfair' inequality. What follows is proposals on income distribution, assets, inheritance and business, that will rebalance the tax system in a 'fair' way, promote meritocracy and reduce inequality between the 1% and the rest.

Income Distribution

As mentioned earlier in this chapter, the living wage has been a fantastic policy implementation for the bottom end of the income spectrum. Linking the living wage to 60% of median income means it will be roughly £9 an hour by 2020. Keeping it at this rate is definitely sustainable if businesses are offered the correct incentives.

In the last two tax years the lower income 20% of the workforce has seen by far the largest pay rise, thus reducing inequality. There is also a case that the National Living Wage should be brought in from the age of 21. Any lower than this, less young people will be hired because of lack of experience. Though I must say my heart is telling me to disagree profoundly with my head as I remember my 17-year-old self at McDonald's getting paid £2 less than a 25-year-old who had just started when I had been there for 18 months.

With the rise in the personal allowance reaching £12,500, this will mean a £1,200 income tax cut per year between 2010–20 under the Conservatives. Taking the poorest workers out of National Insurance if they earn less than £12,500 would further help the lowest incomes as the threshold currently stands at just over £8,100 for PAYE workers. If the threshold was raised to £12,500 it would mean a tax cut worth over £500 a year for all workers on £12,500 and above. This would be a significant tax cut in genuinely taking the lowest paid workers out of direct taxation altogether. With the thresholds equalised, both income tax and National Insurance can be merged to simplify the tax system.

Taxes on fuel are another significant dent into the incomes of people on low to medium wages. Whether this is VAT on fuel bills or VAT/fuel duty on petrol, these ridiculously high taxes need to be cut. We pay some of the highest fuel bills in the world, especially when filling up with petrol and diesel. When fuelling your car, 75% of this cost goes straight to the government and action needs to be taken to reduce this tax.

With the living wage being adopted, if the National Insurance threshold can rise, if fuel bills can be cut; that means that the lowest paid people in society will be paying less tax in the first place therefore justifying limiting welfare payments. The above proposals are in tune with the Conservative belief that taxpayers should be able to keep more of their own money in the first place rather than expecting top ups from the State.

It may not be populist to say so, but I don't think that the highest earners should pay more in direct income tax than they currently do. Keeping the 45p higher rate is crucial to remain competitive in a globalised economy, although I would be uncomfortable if it got dropped down to 40p in the current climate.

The Lefts' 'fake maths' is extraordinary when you hear the Corbynistas or the Green Party naively and misleadingly tirade about the many billions of pounds' worth of tax which can be raised through a wealth tax. Empirically, we have the example of President Hollande who brought in a 75p higher rate of tax for the rich in 2012, which led to thousands of wealth creators leaving France. The policy was soon dropped as less tax was raised from the wealthy. Embarrassingly Hollande not only dropped the tax, he introduced austerity, attempted to liberalise the labour market, therefore destroying the credibility of the Socialist Party of France. Higher direct income taxes on the wealthy are a good way of raising less tax, not more. As I've made clear, I believe that income taxes are high enough. Meritocracy will not be promoted by raising the basic or the higher rate of tax. I will now discuss the issue of assets which in some regards is a very different story.

Housing

Until recently, buying a house was seen as a modest aspiration and a huge driver of social mobility, but in the last 20 years, home ownership has halved for under 25s. I remember watching *Newsnight* several years ago and the presenter Evan Davis stated that for the first time ever there were more people in the UK who had mortgages and paid them off, than those who were actually still paying them. This was a dramatic statement and all governments over the past 30 years have failed on this issue. The housing crisis began with the Right to Buy policy brought in under Margaret Thatcher. This was fundamentally a fantastic policy as many working-class families were given the chance to own their house. Funnily enough, it was the biggest ever redistribution of wealth from the government to the people (not that there were much plaudits from the Left at that time). Even if this policy was the right one, there is no doubt there should have been a part two to this policy i.e. one home should have been built every time one was sold off. With a growing and ageing population we are now in need of many more homes to be built.

Housing inequality is one of the biggest crises that we face as a nation. Investment is crucial in order to challenge this crisis. Harold MacMillan's Conservative Government built 300,000 homes a year in the early 1960s, and with a much larger population we need to be building just as many. Over £9 billion is spent on this part of the Housing Benefit bill, which goes to private landlords who can charge high rents because of the lack of supply in housing. This Housing Benefit bill is over twice the size of the overall housing budget which is the definition of a false economy. We need to use this money much more productively by ploughing it back into building more homes.

We need to build affordable homes for those who are seeking to buy and we need to modernise social housing for those who do not wish to buy. Planning permission needs to be relaxed but of course the vast majority of the greenbelt still needs to be protected. Brownfields should be used to build the majority of new housing and councils should be given the power to borrow in order to build. An all-out offensive on the supply side of housing has to be enforced so young people can buy homes again and many of the lowest income people can afford to rent.

On the demand side, the Conservative Government has brought in good policies on both ends of the housing market but unfortunately this has not been promoted alongside building enough homes. The Help to Buy Scheme was a great policy when the housing market needed a boost as many young people could only save a 5% deposit. The Help to Buy ISA (where potential first time buyers can save £200 a month which is topped up to the tune of 25% by the government) was a helpful initiative when brought in in December 2015.

The Lifetime ISA (where first-time buyers can save £4,000 a year with a 25% government top up) was introduced in April 2017. This should be increased to 50% so many more young people can get their foot on the housing ladder. Starter homes discount of 20% of the market value for first time buyers is another positive initiative.

Finally, the recent proposals of scrapping letting agency fees are welcome and long overdue. I have personally paid over £2,000 in fees in the last six years and when you have to pay for the first month's rent and deposit, paying rip-off fees from letting agencies is the last thing you should have to finance. As explained earlier in this chapter, at the top end of the housing market the Conservative Government sought to take action. This was a move to reduce inequality by bringing in tax disincentives for the wealthiest home owners and second home owners. Stamp duty was hiked and so was the slow removal of tax relief on second home mortgages.

Running in parallel with ramping up the supply side on housing, other changes can be implemented to promote social mobility by helping first-time buyers. Philip Hammond's announcement that stamp duty for first time buyers should not be paid on a home worth up to £300,000 (up from £125,000) is a positive move. This will benefit first-time buyers who live in expensive areas and will allow many younger people to put this extra money saved towards their deposit. Another policy which should be introduced is that those over 60 should be exempt from paying any stamp duty whatsoever on a home if they are wishing to downsize. The charity Independent Age predict that a move like this would encourage elderly people to sell as they may have lacked the immediate funds to pay the stamp duty. They also predict 111,000 family homes could come onto the market as a result.[23]

23 https://www.moneywise.co.uk/news/2017-01-16/retired-downsizers-may-get-stamp-duty-exemption [Accessed 15th March 2017]

As well as stamp duty being further reformed to help the lower end, measures could be taken to put a severe dent in the market at the very top end. With a quick search on Rightmove for properties in London, I found a five-bedroom flat which is on sale for £55 million (April 2017). It's an incomprehensible amount of money for 99% of us. Currently, somebody who buys a home for £1.5 million would pay the same amount of tax than someone who is paying £55 million (12%). There is scope to bring in a higher rate of stamp duty for the most expensive properties. A 25% stamp duty rate on properties over £10 million would ensure the higher end of the housing market slows and the richest 0.5% would pay more in tax when they purchase assets. Another effective way to raise revenue on assets would involve increasing the top council tax band or introducing an additional band.

Inheritance Tax

Many on the Left would like to massively increase inheritance tax as they see the State as having the ultimate authority over somebody's money once they die. Philosophically, the Left believe that the children of the deceased have done nothing to deserve the hard earned money of their parents. To believe in inheritance tax is to believe in perpetual inequality.

The Right believes that if somebody has worked hard and built up assets and income for their children, then this should be allowed to be passed down so they can give their children the best start in life. Opinion polls show us that the public definitely support the Conservative outlook on this tax. This is understandable as you pay taxes throughout your whole life and then you get taxed when you die.

Although I completely understand that it is a normal human instinct to save for your children and pass them your life's earnings/assets, there is scope for making it 'progressive'. Using the word progressive when it comes to inheritance tax seems like an oxymoron but hear me out. The threshold is due to be raised gradually from £325,000 to £1 million by 2020. I completely support this policy but I believe a Conservative Government could take this further. The threshold could be raised to £1.5 million but increase the tax to 45% after this amount.

In the 2017 Spring Budget, probate fees were made more progressive, this meant that the more wealth you passed down, the higher the probate fees would be. This seems to have been proposed in a stealthy way but it ensures that those that pass down the most wealth will see a significant increase in fees.

Business

Being a true believer in a free market where everyone plays by the same rules, the tax differential treatment of small businesses compared to larger businesses can hinder genuine competition. As already stated, corporation tax needs to be low so we can remain a competitive economy where we attract large investors from around the world. In conjunction with this, we need to ensure that the correct taxes are paid. Back in 2016, UK businesses as well as the general public were aghast that George Osborne termed Google paying 3% corporation tax 'a great success'.

The small business owner or even larger outlets like John Lewis can't ring HMRC and attempt to avoid paying even one-sixth of what they owe. To support our small to medium size enterprises we need a freeze on business rates or even a small cut. We don't want our high streets to die as what will replace them? Large digital global corporations make all our lives easier in the way we use the internet but they do not create the same quantity of jobs compared to retail or manufacturing. Business rates in the UK are higher than any property taxes in Europe. We need to support our large and small businesses equally. Both should play by the rules and pay all taxes duly owed.

Improving Capitalism

Capitalism is the best route to growth, prosperity and lifting people out of poverty. The small business owner working 70 hours a week, providing goods to the local community is the backbone of our society. Capitalism plays a huge part in promoting a meritocratic society as somebody can start off at the bottom of a company and work all the way up to the top.

Capitalism gives us the work ethic to get out there and make the best of the talents we have, whilst promoting freedom in the process. Capitalism gives us a reason to get out of bed in the morning and be the best that we can be. Socialism gives us no reason to get out of bed in the morning as we will get paid the same as the hard worker in any case. Below is a socialist experiment in an economics class in the USA. This is a fascinating example of how socialism can never be the answer.

> The professor then said "Ok, we will have an experiment in this class on socialism. All grades would be averaged and everyone would receive the same grade so no one would fail and no one would receive an A".
>
> After the first test the grades were averaged and everyone got a B. The students who studied hard were upset and the students who studied little were happy. But, as the second test rolled around, the students who studied little had studied even less and the ones who studied hard decided they wanted a free ride too; so they studied little...
>
> The second test average was a D! No one was happy. When the third test rolled around the average was an F. The scores never increased as no one would study for anyone else. All failed and the professor told them that socialism would ultimately fail because the harder to succeed, the greater the reward but when a

government takes all the reward away; no one will try or succeed.[24]

Reforming Capitalism

Even though I am sure that socialism can never be the answer, as illustrated through the previous example, if we pro-capitalists are to ensure capitalism survives, there does need to be changes. Working in McDonald's between 2008–13, taught me many useful skills for the modern economy, namely time management, organisation and teamwork. I am proud of the five years I spent working there and overall I learnt a lot, especially the importance of hard work. After working on the tills for my first six months or so, I wanted to work in the kitchen learning how to make the beef and chicken products. At 16 years of age I was earning £4.25 an hour, not a lot of money but it felt like it was to me. When I requested to learn how to work in the kitchen one of the managers told me I could but I had to do it my own time. He told me to clock out after my shift and then I could work in the kitchen unpaid. I stayed on after my shift unpaid several times as I wanted to learn how to make a Big Mac and a Sweet Chilli Chicken Deli.

It was only after a couple of years that I realised how wrong this was. I was advised that I couldn't be paid to learn these extra skills, as labour costs would be too high, but was £4.25 an hour really a lot of money? This was an extreme example and it never happened again after these first few shifts in the kitchen. Apart from this and not being paid any extra for working every Boxing Day and New Year's Eve for three years in a row, I can't have too many complaints about my time at McDonald's. This example does however highlight a wider point. There are serious issues with the way some big businesses operate.

24 http://www.iaindale.com/posts/2017/06/05/if-you-think-labour-s-manifesto-is-fully-costed-read-on [Accessed 18th March 2017]

Big businesses who avoid or evade tax infuriate the Left and should infuriate those of us on the Right even more. Why? Because in some regards it is the antithesis of the essence of capitalism itself. Capitalism is about hard work, entrepreneurship and innovation but above all else it is surely about competition. This is what drives up standards and drives down prices for consumers. If Starbucks are playing 0.01% in corporation tax and John Lewis is paying the full rate of 19%, where is the even playing field for competition?

The tax gap in the UK ranges between £34 billion and £120 billion depending on the source, either of which is a truly appalling amount. Although the current Conservative Government has done more to tackle tax avoidance than any other government, there is clearly much more to be done. An international agreement needs to be reached in order to confront this issue and it should be put back to the top of the agenda as it was several years ago. The diverted profits tax of 25% should be used by the government to prove that although we are a low tax, competitive economy, we still need to make sure all companies pay the correct amount of tax. We should not forget, Adam Smith, the founder of modern free market economics, warned against the market being rigged by big businesses.

In addition to challenging the scourge of tax avoidance and evasion, chief executive pay is another huge bone of contention with the public. Some may be uncomfortable with me raising this subject, but I have surely shown in this book that I am a true believer in free market capitalism. Yet, if the public are to continue to support capitalism, certain elements justifiably need to be reformed.

An opinion poll in 2016 showed a majority of 18–29 year olds in the USA did not support capitalism. This anger against capitalism will be found in far Left groups if Conservatives do not have an answer to the anger which is posed. In the UK between the years 2000–08 FTSE 100 shares dropped by a third. Investors lost a third of their money but executives paid themselves 80% more. This is surely an example of rigging the market. The average pay of FTSE 100 bosses is now 144 times that of the average UK salary. Theresa May's policy initiative of giving shareholders more power to veto this pay will be a bold move and is long overdue. In introducing this policy, she will have the backing of mainstream Conservative opinions from Jesse Norman to Daniel Hannan. Giving shareholders of companies more power than before is a positive capitalist answer to this dilemma.

A New Social Contract

Improving capitalism at the top end of society when it comes to tax avoidance and executive pay is vital if we are to live in a more just society where everyone plays by the same rules. But these two major issues will not in themselves improve meritocracy and the life chances of young people entering into the workforce today. What we need is a new social contract between young people and businesses.

Working as an employability project worker for a charity in Nottingham in 2015, I saw first-hand the positives and negatives of employment in modern Britain. Part of my job was to work in several job centres where I delivered help with CVs, cover letters and interview skills. I met a wide variety of staff and job seekers. The staff did not live up to stereotypes as they were friendly to all job seekers and genuinely wanted to help. I did see a handful of people being sanctioned but this was always because the job seeker had broken their agreement in looking for work. The job seekers were a varied bunch ranging from hard workers who had been made redundant and were struggling with the pace of technological change, to single mothers looking to find their way back into the work place, to teenage boys who thought it was acceptable to come into the job centre stinking of cannabis. Contrary to the nonsense that is spouted by far Left commentators such as

Ken Loach; there was always support at hand in the job centre. This often came in the form of skills and training providers like the Prince's Trust, Babington Group and Remploy.

As well as the positive support offered, there were serious issues with many of the job seekers. They often did not have the self-esteem, communication skills, or basic IT skills to get a job in the modern economy. These lack of skills alongside the negative attitude to work by some, led me to be seriously concerned about the lack of basic employability skills many of our young people have. We need a serious investment programme funded by the private, public and charitable sector to make further inroads on youth unemployment. Low-skilled jobs in general are becoming an ever-increasing problem for the government and this low pay culture will only increase inequality. A low-skilled economy leads to increased zero-hours contracts and agency work. As stated I think much of the media outrage is hyperbole, especially over zero-hours, but undoubtedly these issues persist.

Further support for the self-employed needs to be introduced by the government. Philip Hammond's U-turn following the Budget of 2017 on raising National Insurance for the self-employed was unfortunate, as the announcement was made without a part two which would have strengthened workers' rights. There should have been the introduction of some holiday pay, maternity and paternity rights. With 45% of new jobs created since the 2008 crash being self-employed jobs, this army of 5 million or so workers need to know that the government is on their side for having the gumption to be their own boss. Further support from government in this area will show capitalism can benefit the emerging workforce.

One vital way capitalism can be improved is by supporting a strong trade union movement. Unions at their best work productively with employers to get the best outcomes for the workforce. The Conservatives need to have a more positive message to say to trade unionists and indeed the public sector as a whole. We should be supporting trade unions as they are about individuals getting together collectively to solve workplace issues instead of asking the State to get involved. We should be promoting this unless militant undemocratic actions are being pursued by the unions. In 1979, a scandalous amount of 29 million working days were lost due to industrial action, this figure showed that Margaret Thatcher's reforms were correct. In 2016, after six years of austerity and pay squeezes only 300,000 working days were lost to strike action. Britain is a hard-working nation and the Conservatives need to show the public sector that it is appreciated. It is the public sector who look after us when we are ill, teach us when we are young and keep our country safe and secure.

However, it's not all doom and gloom for the Conservatives over the public sector vote. At the 2015 General Election 33% of the public sector voted Conservative and 36% Labour. This was a small lead for Labour and if we can revitalise our relationship with the public sector through actions to increase social mobility, we can overtake them.

Examples of these improvements could be giving teachers a significant pay rise in the worst performing schools in the country. This would attract the most talented teachers to move to the area and be financially incentivised to help close the attainment gap. When it comes to supporting the future of the NHS and social care, the government could invest in a 'carer to nurse' training scheme, with loans and support so that the ever growing mass of carers can aspire to be nurses. Investment in a job guarantee scheme for soldiers who leave the army after eight years would be a great way of properly honouring the military covenant.

Instead of revitalising the Conservatives relationship with the public sector, the 2017 General Election saw the party go backwards and we are now further behind Labour. This result clearly shows that as well as the innovative schemes as mentioned above, the public sector pay cap should be lifted after seven long years of restraint. If the Conservatives can put policies such as these into practice, we can once again challenge to become the party of the public sector.

The Future: Brexit Rebalancing

With the 23rd June 2016 vote to leave the European Union, we have an historic opportunity to rebalance our economy and change our country for the better. As we prepare to divorce from the EU, leave the customs union and single market, we can look forward to a bright future where we are the masters of our own destiny. Instead of being saddled to the EU's declining share in the world economy, we can become a truly global Britain.

We will be able to strike free trade deals with the fastest growing countries around the world without being shackled to the EU's inability to do so. With the pound fluctuating we can increase our exports dramatically and see a manufacturing revival. Taking back control of our immigration policy means that we will be able to stop the depression of wages at the lower end of the income spectrum.

This is remarkably similar to what the Labour Manifesto stated in 2017 and we should bring them into the negotiations as they too claim they want to leave the single market and seek a free trade deal with the EU. By doing this we would call Labour's bluff on Europe and if they declined they would be exposed as opportunists.

As we prepare to leave the EU, I am certain our International Trade Secretary, Liam Fox, will get Britain into shape for the 2020s by negotiating free trade deals with the likes of the USA, India and China. As Andrea Leadsom said during the BBC EU debate, "Twenty-eight countries couldn't organise a take away together never mind negotiate a free trade deal".[25] It took seven years to complete one with Canada, which is shocking considering how similar the economies are.

---

25 *BBC EU Debate*, Andrea Leadsom, 21st June 2016.

Due to the vested interests of each and every EU country, this will inevitably hold up any deals. This point was proved when a region in Belgium was allowed to hinder the Canadian free trade deal in October 2016 and was a massive embarrassment for the EU. It will be so much simpler for the UK going forward when negotiating global free trade deals, however we should work hard to get a free trade deal with the EU as well. If the EU reject this and choose to punish German car workers and French wine makers to take forward their political ideology, then this would be a calamitous act of self-harm. Though I am confident that the EU will see sense and the UK can indeed have its cake and eat it. After all we will be their largest export market after we leave.

The United Kingdom is the country who began the industrial revolution over 200 years ago. We have a history of creating the greatest inventions and products and exporting them around the world. For over a decade now, politicians have often spoken about rebalancing the economy from consumer spending to manufacturing. The reality of this rhetoric has been very different. Manufacturing halved in the UK under the last Labour Government. In the 1970s it contributed 25% of GDP and now it is only 10% of GDP. Even after this drop, we are still in the top ten when it comes to the largest manufacturing countries in the world. With the UK car industry exporting more cars than ever before, it is the jewel in the British manufacturing crown. With the value of the pound dropping against the dollar and the euro, it means that UK exports have become more competitive abroad. This will boost manufacturing and we can expect to see a healthy rebalancing in our economy. With a stronger manufacturing sector in Britain, many more skilled well-paid jobs will be created. Training up young people and investing in apprenticeships means that manufacturing will be on the upward trend in a post-Brexit Britain.

Immigration reform is imperative post-Brexit if we are to help the lowest paid from being undercut. Many on the

Left refuse to recognise there is a problem in this area as they choose political correctness over helping the lowest earners in society. It's very simple economics, if there is an oversupply of labour in the market then wages will flatline or decline. In effect, support of mass immigration means support for a race to the bottom. This has been the case since 2004 when citizens of the Eastern European countries were entitled to travel to Britain in their millions to work. I worked with dozens of Eastern Europeans at McDonald's and they were great people and some of the hardest workers. Nonetheless I did often think there were many unemployed British people who could be doing the job. It is easy to be a well-meaning supporter of freedom of movement if it doesn't affect your chances of getting a job.

We will still need some low-skilled migration post-Brexit but it does need to be substantially reduced. With leaving the EU we will be able to control the quality and quantity of people entering the country. Lower unskilled migration will mean less people competing for lower skilled jobs. Therefore, employers will have to start paying lower income workers more as there will no longer be an ever increasing abundance of applicants.

The current Conservative Government should not simply be defined as the government who took Britain out of the EU. We should aim to rebalance our economy, renew our society and increase social mobility. This chimes with Conservative philosophy of equality of opportunity not equality of outcome. In Britain today we are a long way from a meritocracy as privately educated individuals still dominate the majority of the most highly paid professional jobs.

Theresa May knows that the government has a major role to play in confronting this endemic problem and promoting social mobility in the process. There are economic leavers that the government has at its disposal to reduce inequality and build a more meritocratic society. Social reform is similarly crucial in this regard and this is what I will now to turn to.

3 Education

"Our education system should help children out of the circumstances in which they were born, not lock them into the circumstances in which they were born. We need them to fly as high as their luck, their ability and sheer hard graft can take them."[26]

– John Major, 2013

Introduction

Growing up in Northern Ireland at the beginning of this century, the binary system of grammar schools and secondary moderns were still in place. If you could pass the 11 Plus, then you had one chance to leave your social background and go to a fantastic school with aspiration and academic rigour. The problem was, if you were not in the top 20% then you attended a secondary modern where the teaching quality, resources available and expected aspirations were the opposite of a grammar education. In 2003, I comprehensively failed my 11 Plus as I did not become somewhat academic until a much later age.

If I had passed my 11 Plus I would have attended Regent House Grammar School. My life would have been dramatically different as I would have attended one of the

26 John Major speech, South Norfolk constituency party, 10th November 2013.

highest performing schools in the United Kingdom. Instead I ended up at Movilla High School which was the opposite to Regent in terms of aspiration and academic achievement. The contrast between the two schools is extraordinary and shows that the failure of one exam can have severe consequences for a child's life chances. My formative years in the education system is probably the reason why I have always been fascinated with social mobility.

In 2010, the most controversial radical Education Secretary, Michael Gove, understood that education in many ways is the key driver to improving social mobility. Adopted as a child by working-class Labour supporters from Aberdeen, he earned a scholarship to a private school and ended up at Oxford. Coming from his background he clearly believed that any child could succeed given the right education. This has motivated the Conservatives in driving through some of the most sweeping, decentralising reforms throughout the years since 2010. Overall, I am an advocate of these education reforms but in my analysis I will not shy away from pointing out the mistakes made along the way during this transformation. Teachers were not inspired by the Conservatives vision as it was poorly explained and the tone was too dismissive of their important views.

We are still a long way from having one of the most meritocratic education systems in the world and I plan to further explore ways forward. From children's centres to school funding to university, education is one of the most dominant parts of all our lives growing up. There should be an appropriate school for vocational learners as well as the more academic, the reforms which have introduced choice and competition can help ensure every child has a good school place.

As Conservatives we have many proud achievements in education policy but the General Election of 2017 has shown us that we need to start engaging with young people around issues such as tuition fees and the larger issue of debt. In this chapter I aim to tackle concerns with Conservative education policy but in addition to this offer bold policy solutions, which will further improve education for the most disadvantaged children.

1997–2010: Inheritance from Labour

The Conservatives rightly criticised the education policy under New Labour as the UK slipped down the OECD's (PISA) world rankings on academic standards, but somewhat paradoxically they sought to build on many of the reforms which Blair embarked upon during his third term. Labour's overall performance in government showed that social mobility cannot simply be enhanced by throwing money at a particular area of government spending. For example, despite huge increases in public spending under the Blair/Brown Governments, we fell dramatically down the world league tables for reading and writing. The UK was 8th in the world in the year 2000, by 2009 we had slipped to 25th.

This dramatic drop down the world rankings led to the accusation of grade inflation as GCSE and A level results seemed to rise every year at the same time as the UK's world standing dropped. By 2008, after 11 years of New Labour, nearly half of children entering into secondary school at age 11 fell below the expected standard in literacy and numeracy.[27] Education performance amongst the most disadvantaged remained low under New Labour and it undoubtedly contributed to the stalling of social mobility.

In his final years as prime minister, Tony Blair envisaged structural reforms to England's education system to turn around failing schools and deliver on his top priority when he entered government of 'education, education, education'. Alongside his policy advisor Andrew Adonis, they developed

27 Matt Beech and Simon Lee, *Ten Years of New Labour*, Palgrave Macmillan, 2008.

independent state schools, calling them academies. These schools were to be completely state funded and free to students, but would be much more independent of local authority control. Freedoms included setting their own pay and conditions for staff, curriculum delivery and the ability to change the length of terms and school days.

The argument for academies was to give people more choice through competition and ultimately this would put pressure on the whole education system to improve its performance. David Cameron used his first Prime Minister's Questions to support this policy but Labour faced a backlash from its own party as it was seen to undermine the universalism of state education.

The introduction of academies proved to be helping the most disadvantaged young people as two independent studies of pre-2010 showed exams were improving and in addition they were having positive impacts on the performance of neighbouring schools. By 2010 under Labour's academies, GCSE results were improving far faster than both the national average and schools with similar pupil intakes. These GCSE results achieved through choice and competition encouraged the Conservatives to put 'rocket boosters' on the academy programme when they entered government in 2010.

The Gove Revolution: Education Since 2010

Before explaining how Michael Gove and the Coalition Government revolutionised schools in England; positive reforms and government intervention on childcare deserves examination. Well-funded and high quality childcare is crucial as this has a monumental impact on how well a child does at school in later years. In 2011 an OECD report documented the growing burden of childcare. It showed that 25 hours of nursery care for a child under two cost an average of £5,000 per year, rising to £6,000 in London[28].

28 OECD, *Family Database*, 2011.

Parents in Britain were shown to have higher childcare costs as a share of income than any other country in the OECD, spending an average of 33% of net income on childcare. The Conservatives in government pursued policies to combat this issue including the offer of 15 hours' free childcare a week for the lowest paid parents of two year olds. This led to 40% of the poorest two-year-olds receiving funded childcare places. In 2016 the government started to roll out the 30 hours a week free childcare for three- and four-year-olds and despite teething issues over delivery, it is a fantastic initiative. In addition to free childcare, the 'early years' Pupil Premium' was introduced. This meant that a set amount of money is given to the most disadvantaged three- and four-year-olds to help them be school ready at the age of five.

With the majority of five-year-olds eligible for free school meals not being school ready, this extra funding is imperative to improve social mobility going forward. Studies have shown that school readiness at the age of five has a strong impact on future educational attainment and life chances. The Conservatives record on early years' education has been positive as Ofsted acknowledged in 2015. They stated that early years' education in Britain has 'never been stronger', with 85% of early years' settings considered Good or Outstanding.[29] The report also showed significant progress for the most disadvantaged children, which shows the extra childcare and Pupil Premium have been policy successes for early years' education. If this positive upturn can be sustained, in a decade's time social mobility will have a good chance of increasing in the UK as the quality of early years' education has improved.

29 Ofsted, 'Early education is better than ever but attainment gap remains', 13th July 2015.

School Reforms

The Coalition entered into government seeking to build on Labour's school reforms and rejected the traditional policy solution for Conservatives when debating social mobility and education, namely grammar schools. Cameron thought that New Labour's school reforms were a better answer to improved social mobility than a return to school selection at the age of 11.

In a 2007 speech, Cameron called opposition to grammar schools a 'key test' of whether the Conservative Party was fit for office.[30] Instead, the 2010 Conservative Manifesto focused on building new academies (free schools) in deprived areas, a continuation of the policies of the previous government. Michael Gove led the charge on this front and firmly believed creating choice and competition could drive up standards. The ultimate goal was to ensure that future Cabinets could be dominated by state schooled students and not just the privately educated. This would be achieved through high standards and radical reform, not social engineering. As Gove had been adopted, he understood that where you come from should not define where you are going in life.

Academy expansion and free schools were the structural reforms Gove put in place to improve learning and social mobility in England. These radical reforms gave teachers, parents, charities and businesses the power to set up their own school, free of local authority control. This move away from a 'one size fits all' strategy encouraged innovation and creativity when improving children's learning.

When the Coalition took office there were only 200 academies in England but by 2016 there were over 4000. Most of these are secondary school academies, and they are now the majority over local authority maintained establishments. Many national standards still remained as any new school

30 http://news.bbc.co.uk/1/hi/uk_politics/6679005.stm [Accessed 30th March 2017]

which opened still had to teach a 'broad and balanced curriculum' and they were still inspected by Ofsted. Even so, there is clear independence from the local authority.

Although academies are independent, when Gove was Education Secretary he encouraged learning based on facts, history and literature. During his four years as Education Secretary, GCSE exams and the curriculum were made more difficult for young people in an attempt to raise standards. This upset many teaching professionals who saw this type of learning as too rigid. Although many of these reforms have been unpopular, going back to the PISA tests, in 2016 England showed clear improvement in Maths, English and Science. Though the UK's overall score was dragged down by Scotland and Wales which had not followed Gove's reforms. Studies on academies show that they achieve slightly better GCSE results than local authority schools but it will still take another decade to truly see the fruits of these reforms when it comes to social mobility.

One of the greatest innovations under the Conservatives has been the Pupil Premium, a policy which has received little media coverage. This was introduced in 2011 and amounts to an extra £2.5 billion annual investment in the most disadvantaged children in England. Schools with children on either free school meals or are in local authority care are each given a grant which seeks to close the attainment gap. At the time the government argued that this would mean schools would want to admit more disadvantaged children and it would incentivise free schools to open in deprived areas. This was effectively the 'marketisation' of the school system as schools were incentivised to compete for poorer pupils.

It will take several more years to truly test the success of the Pupil Premium in improving social mobility but results so far seem positive. Those on free school meals are still half as likely as their better off peers to achieve five good GCSEs (A*–C) but progress has been made. The success rate of children on free school meals achieving five good GCSEs has jumped from 18% in 2005 to over 33% in 2016. This is positive progress but the attainment gap is still far too wide if we are going to live in a society based on merit. It is still the case that average-ability children from wealthy families on average overtake high-ability children from poor families by the time they sit their GCSEs. This is unjustifiable and shows why we need to bring the idea of a meritocracy back to the forefront of the national political debate.

Case studies have shown that the Pupil Premium has often been significant when earmarked for spending on disadvantaged pupils or to help schools to support these pupils. Working in a job overseeing the educational progress of children in care, I have seen this first hand on numerous occasions. Each child in care is given a £1,900 per annum Pupil Premium grant which resides with either their school or the local authority. This can be used to close the attainment gap in so many ways. It can fund extra tuition for a child who may have missed a lot of school because of lack of stability growing up and has consequently moved from area to area. I have seen this extra funding for tuition for dozens of young people in care. As well as academic achievement, I have seen the Pupil Premium be used for cultural activities for young people, whether it be for music lessons or educational trips. If the Pupil Premium funding was not there for children in care, there is no doubt the attainment gap would widen between the poorest young people and the rest.

School Reform Failures

Breaking up the government's monopoly of schools was always going to be controversial with teaching unions and local authorities as power was decentralised. The teaching unions have a history of opposing any reform under any government and paradoxically they have always been the small c conservatives. A decade ago, Tony Blair spoke of the 'forces of conservatism' and public sector 'wreckers.'[31] Even New Labour's reforms were opposed by the educational establishment so the Conservatives were never going to have an easy ride.

Unfortunately, Michael Gove made it easy for them to oppose the government's policies by referring to them as the 'blob'. Gove could have done much more to explain his radical vision and improve his tone to keep teachers onside. In February 2013 the Association of Teachers and Lecturers passed a motion of 'no confidence' against Gove. Two months later the National Union of Teachers did the same, the first time in its 143-year history.

After four years, David Cameron felt he had to remove Gove as Education Secretary as it was costing the Conservatives a lot of votes. The Conservative leadership were clearly supportive of Gove's radical policies but sought a more consensual education secretary to carry them forward. As I've shown, academies and free schools are a fantastic idea but teachers were not sold the vision and the public were not included in the debate, therefore not able to get on board with the government's policies.

Gove's revolutionary tendencies led to many problems when attempting to deliver reforms and contributed in alienating teachers. In 2012 he planned to abolish GCSEs and return to the O-level system. At the same time, he had ideas for an English Baccalaureate Certificate overseen by a single examination board. In 2013, Gove had to pull back from this, stating it was 'a bridge too far'. In the end, instead of abolishing GCSEs he made them more stringent and reformed the national curriculum to focus more on knowledge based learning. With the free school programme being rolled out, it is easy to see why other reforms were difficult to implement at the same time.

31 http://www.independent.co.uk/news/blair-pledges-to-purge-britain-of-the-forces-of-conservatism-1122916.html [Accessed 4th April 2017]

Even these reforms were up for debate as the free school programme was based on the profit-making schools in Sweden. Gove wished to see free schools make profits so they could expand further but this was ruled out as many in the Coalition Government did not want to see the commercialisation of a public service. Even when the Conservative majority government was elected in 2015, none of these controversial school reforms were put back on the agenda. Although, another controversial reform was announced by George Osborne in his March 2016 Budget, forcing all schools to become academies. This went against the very concept of academies as they were designed to 'free' schools, forcing all schools to be academies proved to be very unpopular with backbench Conservatives and was dropped in May 2016.

Universities

I was in my first year at university when in November 2010, the Coalition Government tripled tuition fees from just over £3,000 to £9,000 a year. I remember the protests all over the country, the perceived unfairness and the fury of many current and future students. At the time, I was instinctively against this rise, thinking the scale of debt was deeply unfair. This was just before 'I saw the light' as I was to become a Conservative supporter several months later. I remember speaking to the Socialist Workers Party in Sheffield about the rise in fees and we fully agreed on lambasting this 'rich, elitist Tory Government'. Of course I no longer believe in the simplicity of the Left's argument and although I still have conflicting views over tuition fees, it's important to analyse this issue in a rational way, focusing primarily on its impact in relation to social mobility.

History of Tuition Fees

Many students who argue against tuition fees base their cause on former students 'back in the day' not having to pay anything. Back in the mid-1960s, only 10% of people progressed onto higher education which meant free education would be affordable if only a tiny elite were able to go. At this time, there were very few young working-class people able to succeed in reaching university. As well as fees being free for the students of the 1960s, they were given grants worth nearly £6,000 a year to live at university. Therefore, a lot of taxpayer's money was given to a relatively small group of students.

By the 1990s the Conservatives and Labour wished to move away from this system and supported the mass participation of young people entering university. Tony Blair even set a target of 50% of young people attending university. With such a steep increase in the number of students attending university, there needed to be a new system that ensured its affordability and sustainability. In 1998, David Blunkett introduced tuition fees of £1,000 a year and made the argument that as those who attend university earn more than those who don't, they should pay something towards their education. Only the better off students would pay for these fees as the poorer students would be subsidised. Critics argued that as a higher educated workforce benefits the whole of society, it should be paid for out of general taxation.

To ensure the sustainability of higher education, in 2004 Labour tripled tuition fees to £3,000 (a fact which the current generation of students seems to have forgotten). This was in direct contradiction to the 2001 Labour manifesto which promised not to introduce 'top up fees'. Luckily for them, students were much more forgiving at the 2005 General Election than they would be ten years later with the Liberal Democrats.

New Labour proposed that graduates were to make a contribution of 9% of their salary when they earned over £15,000 a year. Graduates who would not reach this threshold would never pay anything back; if their wage dropped below this threshold they would cease to pay. It was a form of graduate tax but it was a defined contribution instead of an open-ended sum. Labour argued that this tripling of tuition fees was progressive as some of this money raised would be used to introduce grants for poorer students. Three years after Labour introduced the new system, university life was still being dominated by the middle classes, however evidence showed that it was not putting off poorer students from accessing higher education.

Coalition Tripling of Fees

During the middle of the recession in 2009, the then Labour Business Secretary, Peter Mandelson, set up a review into funding higher education. He planned to overhaul tuition fees and treat students more like customers. Setting up the Browne Review[32] (which conveniently would be published after the 2010 General Election), Mandelson stressed the commitment of improving social mobility for the disadvantaged.

Throughout the 2010 General Election, the Conservatives and Labour both opaquely stated they would consider the results of the Browne Review. Infamously, in a bold move to target the student vote, the Liberal Democrats pledged to abolish tuition fees altogether. Little did they know they would be in government several weeks later with the country spending over £150 billion a year more than it was raising in tax. Suddenly this unfunded spending pledge didn't look so easy to deliver.

The Liberal Democrat pledge to abolish tuition fees was a hangover from their days as a party of protest. Under Clegg they became a party of government which had to make tough decisions. Before the 2010 election Clegg had tried and failed

32 Department for Business, Innovation and Skills, *Securing a sustainable future for higher education: an independent review of higher education funding and student finance [Browne report]*, 12th October 2010.

to persuade the Liberal Democrat Policy Committee to drop the party's opposition to tuition fees and instead focus on bursaries for the less affluent. The problem with this was many who supported the Liberal Democrats wanted higher education to be free as they believed it would improve social mobility.

Even with Clegg attempting to change the policy, he still endorsed a statement by the National Union of Students committing parliamentary candidates to: 'Vote against any increase in fees in the next parliament'. He was then photographed with this pledge, a photograph which haunted him for the rest of his political career.

In October 2010 the Browne Review was released and sent shockwaves throughout universities. It proposed lifting the tuition fees cap entirely so that universities could charge whatever they deemed necessary. Crucially, the report recommended raising the threshold before graduates started paying back their fees from £15,000 to £21,000, there would be no upfront fees and part-time students would be eligible for loans to pay for tuition fees. The report speculated that only the top 40% of earners would pay all their fees back (as the debt is written off after 30 years) and the lowest 20% of earners would pay less than under the previous threshold of £15,000.

Before the government's response to the Browne Review, a graduate tax was considered by Vince Cable and even George Osborne. But they soon concluded it lacked flexibility and may leave universities underfunded. In November 2010, the government endorsed the starting threshold of £21,000 but did not abolish the cap altogether, settling on a limit of £9,000 per annum. A week later 50,000 student demonstrators marched through London against the planned rise in fees, 200 of whom broke into Conservative headquarters and vandalised the building. The demonstrators shouted 'Tory Scum' as they protested against what is by any measure a progressive tax on middle-class graduates. Even if some understood this, it was the sheer amount of debt which worried so many, admittedly this included myself.

Deterring the Disadvantaged?

Tuition fees is a visceral subject for many students who resent the fact that the generation which have come before have 'pulled up the ladder of opportunity'. But with the number of young people going to university increasing nearly tenfold since the 1960s, reform was always going to be necessary. When tuition fees were trebled under Labour in 2004 and trebled again under the Coalition in 2010, many feared this would lead to less disadvantaged young people attending university. In reality the opposite has been true. Since tuition fees were trebled, record numbers of students from disadvantaged backgrounds have entered university as there continues to be no upfront costs. A report has shown that 'young people from the poorest areas are now 43% more likely to go to university than they were in 2009–10'.[33] This evidence shows that raising tuition fees has not had a detrimental impact when it comes to social mobility and attending university.

In Scotland, there are no tuition fees but this has ended up being a huge tax cut for the middle classes. It is ignored by the media that a disadvantaged young person from England is twice as likely to attend university than somebody with the same background from Scotland. Since the rise of tuition fees there clearly has been an effort by English universities to help lower income students gain access to higher education. An example of this is children in care being given leeway on grades at most universities.

What is clear from any objective calculation is that with the repayment threshold raised from £15,000 to £21,000, only the most successful graduates will pay their loan off.

33 Jo Johnson speech, Higher Education sector at Reform, Thursday 20 July 2017.

Under the £15,000 repayment threshold, the Institute of Fiscal Studies predicted that the 30 year write off meant that 32% of graduates would have some debt written off. Under the £21,000 repayment threshold, 73% will have at least some debt written off.[34] This much higher figure suggests a false economy on fees as the vast majority of students won't pay it off.

A simple tax calculation shows that a graduate would have to be in a high-earning job throughout their career to pay off their student loan. For example, somebody who earns on average £35,000 throughout a 30-year career would still not get anywhere near paying off their student loan. I never heard this sort of argument when I was at university. Students clearly but understandably could not get past the fact that the sheer amount of debt you end up with is overwhelming.

34 Institute for Fiscal Studies, Payback time? Student debt and loan repayments: what will the 2012 reforms mean for graduates?, April 2014.

Moving Forward: Future Education Reforms

Improving social mobility through education policy is a perpetual battle we will always face as a nation. But for things to really change for the better we need to not only use government as a tool, we need society to become more aspirational collectively. Why shouldn't every parent want to send their child to a Good or Outstanding Ofsted rated school? Why shouldn't every child from a council estate want to aspire to go to university? Why shouldn't a working-class couple who work at McDonald's want their child to attend Oxford?

Aspiration should be at the heart of our education policy but we need a national campaign to entrench this. Chinese children on free school meals show aspiration is crucial. When it comes to GCSEs they still get better results than the national average. They are only marginally behind Chinese children who do not claim free school meals.[35] Too often it is a poverty of ambition that holds many of us back, not having a low income in its itself.

Materialism and overnight fame is a dangerous goal for many children, as this is mostly unrealistic. A generation ago, the most popular career aspirations for children was banking and teaching. Unfortunately, these aspirations are not as popular as before, being an actor, popstar or a sportsman are now top of this list. We need to once again show that the best way to move up the social ladder is through hard work, not a quick fix.

To help turn this rhetoric of aspiration into reality, we need policies to back up the campaign. Investment in careers advisors is crucial to this. Many schools have cut back on careers advisors and I know from my job working with children in care that professional objective advice is crucial

35 Kwasi Kwarteng, Priti Patel, Dominic Raab, Chris Skidmore and Elizabeth Truss, *Britannia Unchained: Global Lessons for Growth and Prosperity*', Palgrave Macmillan, 2012.

for a teenager. Alongside investment in careers, schools should invest in financial and business classes; linking in with local businesses and universities.

Encouraging the children of today to be the private sector buccaneers of tomorrow is a sound investment in the future. In tangent with educational opportunities to improve aspiration, there needs to be further support in school for children with mental health issues. Self-harming, online bullying and depression blights too many children in Britain today and it's a national scandal. A child's health as well as their education is crucial when encouraging them to be the best that they can be.

Improving Schools

The New Labour and Conservative Governments have improved schools considerably by allowing for a greater diversity of school provisions. This in turn has increased parental choice and market incentives have even been used to encourage schools to compete for children on free school meals, e.g. the Pupil Premium. But the fact remains that a child is 27 times more likely to attend an inadequate school if they are from a poor background. There is still a lack of 'equality of opportunity' as the most deprived areas have 30% fewer good schools than the least deprived.

There is a lack of good teachers who want to work in these deprived areas. We need to attract the best teachers to close the attainment gap, reduce unfair inequality and promote social mobility. In the bottom fifth performing local authorities we need to see higher pay for teachers so they are more open to working in the most challenging schools. Teachers should be in it for the outcomes not the incomes, but in reality those working with the most difficult children should be incentivised to do so.

The Return of Grammars

When discussing education and social mobility, many on the political Right often cite grammars as a solution for the most disadvantaged to rise to the top. After being soundly rejected under David Cameron, one of Theresa May's first policy initiatives was the creation of new grammar schools in England.

Many on the Right argue grammars gave working-class and lower-middle-class children the chance to receive the best academic education and to challenge independent schools. Some figures do back this up, i.e. by the end of the 1960s, 38% of places were afforded to privately educated pupils at Oxford. The proportion is now back up to nearly 50%. Many on the Left argue that old grammar schools (just like those today) were overwhelmingly dominated by middle-class children and most of the working class attended secondary moderns.

Other major criticisms include forcing children to sit a test at the age of 11, the result of which would define the opportunities available to them. Those who wish to praise grammar schools may have good reasons to do so, on the other hand, no one wishes to praise secondary moderns where 80% of children used to end up.

As mentioned at the beginning of this chapter, the grammar school debate is deeply personal to me as I failed my 11 Plus in 2003. Instead of attending a top performing grammar school, I attended a school which by any measure would be placed in the bottom 1% in the UK. I remember the lack of aspiration from the pupils, the constant inflow of supply teachers and the gangs which were widespread throughout my five years there. Admittedly I was often in the thick of much of the disruption caused and I estimate that I received a couple of hundred detentions throughout my time there (the vast majority before my GCSE years). Until I reached the age of 15, I was too often getting myself in trouble with teachers rather than showing aspiration to do well in my GCSEs.

Luckily, I managed to 'wise up' in my last year of school and achieved 7 GCSEs A*–C. Roughly five out of 160 pupils in my year managed to get into a sixth form (obviously Movilla didn't have one) and eventually go to university. I was one of the lucky ones who achieved this as only about 20% of my school year achieved 5 GCSEs or more A*–C. Conversely, 98% of Regent Grammar School pupils achieved 5 GCSEs A*–C.

I don't want to personally criticise the teachers at Movilla but the culture of mediocrity (at best) is difficult to ignore. A school which didn't even offer English Literature as a GCSE is extraordinary; I only found out how odd this was several years later when I attended university. Unfortunately, since I left Movilla in 2008 the school has gone further downhill. By 2016, the BBC reported that there had been more detentions in the previous year than there had been pupils. In addition to this the number of children leaving the school with five GCSEs A*–C had dropped to 18.4% and inspectors reported that the quality of education was Inadequate.[36]

Should there be a return to grammar schools to promote social mobility for some? You may presume that with my personal background I would be viscerally opposed to such a move. As well as the above criticisms, many of the poorest families have chaotic lives, thus giving a potential taker of the 11 Plus a severe disadvantage over a middle-class child with two parents still at home. The middle-class child can often rely on tuition being paid for so they pass the 11 Plus on the day; the lower income family cannot afford such a luxury. Nor do global comparisons promote grammar schools as nine out of the ten of the best education systems in the world are comprehensive.

---

36 http://www.bbc.co.uk/news/uk-northern-ireland-35417136 [Accessed 4th April 2017]

Ultimately, I think it would be a dreadful mistake to return to the grammar schools of the past as it inherently favours those who come from more stable backgrounds. They can entrench inequality and for those who fail the 11 Plus it can damage self-esteem in a long-term manner. If those who claim grammars promote social mobility really believe this, there are ways to introduce them to genuinely focus on giving the poorest children a leg up in life. As a Conservative I believe choice and strong competition is crucial to promote social mobility so I do think there should be some trials of new grammars to see if they can work but there does need to be some serious changes from the old system.

First, I would change the 11 Plus as it is a basic fact that many children develop at different ages, including myself. This could be changed to an exam which could be set at the age of 14 and where retakes could be taken if needed. Second, only open them in the most disadvantaged areas, i.e. the bottom 20% of performing local authorities. This would show that the reintroduction of grammars is to help the poorest, not cement middle-class privilege.

Third, alongside introducing academic selection, ensure that there is selection when it comes to favouring low income households. At least 75% of children who attend the new grammars would have to come from families who earn less than £30,000 a year, at least 40% would have to be on free school meals. Current grammar schools have an abysmally low amount of children on free school meals and any new system would need to quickly rectify this. I understand that many would be put off by such radical proposals but if we are to take the grammar school and social mobility argument seriously, suggestions such as these should be considered.

Those who are critical of grammar schools think that selection by ability is abhorrent but I never hear commentators criticise the current system of selection by income and house price. Homes in areas with good schools are substantially more expensive than in areas with less desirable schools. In 2015, a detailed survey showed that parents would pay 18% more for a property near their preferred school – the equivalent of £32,000.[37] A report by Sutton Trust has shown that the top 500 state-funded schools have less than half the national average amount of children eligible for free school meals.[38] This fact is not included in the national debate as the narrative is always the perceived unfairness of selection by ability, not selection by income. In any case the grammar school debate has been put on hold after the failure of the Conservatives to win a majority at the 2017 General Election.

Technical Skills

Often overlooked from the 1944 Education Act[39] which created grammar schools and secondary moderns, was the mention of technical schools. This 'tripartite' system was meant to cater for all needs, academic and vocational. It recognised that children had different abilities but all could be successful. Unfortunately, the reality was that few technical schools were built and the vast majority of the time it was a binary choice between grammar and secondary schools. Technical schools could have been a great enhancer of social mobility if they were built but the vast majority of working-class children ended up in secondary moderns instead.

A recent initiative to promote technical education is the creation of University Technical Colleges. UTCs are free schools which have to be led by sponsor universities. They are non-selective but as they require a university sponsor they are distinctive from other free schools. Students aged 14–19

---

37 https://www.theguardian.com/education/2015/sep/02/one-in-four-families-move-house-to-secure-school-place-survey [Accessed 8th April 2017]

38 https://www.theguardian.com/education/2013/jun/03/top-state-schools-socially-exclusive [Accessed 8th April 2017]

39 The Education Act 1944. [Accessed 8th April 2017]

can attend a UTC as they can offer technical courses to those who would prefer this route. Beginning at 14 is an innovative new way of taking into account that some teenagers develop at different ages. As the curriculum is technical, UTCs recruit young people when their talents and interests are further developed. From manufacturing to engineering, creative arts to media, there is a variety of different UTCs available across the country.

Progress seems to have stalled somewhat in recent years as there has been an issue with student numbers at UTCs. My only explanation is that this must be a branding or marketing issue as a great many children would love to attend a UTC, especially as so many are technically gifted but don't always have the opportunity at a mainstream school to develop their skills.

Under New Labour, the race to get 50% of young people to attend university clearly led to a 'forgotten 50%' of those who did not wish to attend university. Under the Coalition Government a culture of apprenticeships was brought back to Britain. Over 2.5 million apprenticeships have been created in Britain as vocational training has returned to the forefront of the government's post-16 policies. The most popular vocations have not been in the traditional industries of manufacturing, engineering or construction but in the growing sectors of business administration, health and retail.

In seeking to bring back traditional technical training, the government introduced 'T-Levels' at the 2017 Spring Budget. This is a complete overhaul of technical education which will focus on 15 sectors. As well as recent popular vocational opportunities like social care, crucially, there will be a focus on sectors like digital, construction, engineering, manufacturing and transport. This £500 million annual investment seeks to tackle the UK's productivity problem and help create a higher skilled economy where there are much more well-paid jobs.

Education and Social Mobility

If we are to radically improve social mobility in this country, we need to look at who is rising to the top in Britain today. The Coalition Government's school reforms will take some years to measure but further reform is necessary to give the poorest young people a chance to get on in life. As previously illustrated, the raising of tuition fees has not deterred the most disadvantaged from going to university, but this somewhat masks the fact that the top Russell Group universities remain out of reach for the poorest.

In recent years there have been reports that only 1% of Oxford's intake had free school meals, with at least 15% of children claiming free school meals this is an astonishing figure. At the same time pupils who attend fee-paying schools are five times more likely to study at Oxford than their peers in the state sector. Russell Group universities need to do much more to open up places to those from lower income backgrounds and take into account if they went to a poor performing school. In addition, the 2016 government consultation on schools suggested much more work needs to be done by universities and private schools sponsoring and improving academies in their local area. This needs to be enacted as soon as possible to raise standards for all and strengthen the chances of the poorest children attending the top universities.

The glass ceiling for those young people from the lowest income backgrounds, doesn't end if they fail to get into a top university, it follows that many professions are automatically out of reach. A report showed that top employers recruit from an average of only 20 out of 115 universities.[40] Another report gave examples of the lack of people from working-class origins in certain professions. This included only 4% of doctors, 6% of barristers and 11% of journalists. While

40 Social Mobility and Child Poverty Commission, *State of the Nation 2014 Report*, 20th October 2014.

Oxford and Cambridge graduates comprise just 1% of Britain's population, according to a recent report they make up 75% of senior judges and 59% of cabinet ministers.[41] Of course you would expect a high percentage of the top professions being from the top two universities, but this is extraordinarily excessive.

Nothing has been more detrimental to excluding those from modest backgrounds to the top professions than unpaid internships. In professions like law and the media unpaid internships can only be afforded by the parents of middle-class young people. Somebody from a low income background in Doncaster could never afford to move to London to complete an unpaid internship.

In 2016, the Conservative MP Alec Shelbrooke introduced a bill to parliament seeking to ban unpaid internships, labelling them "the acceptable face of unpaid labour in modern Britain". His bill was defeated by the government. If the Conservatives are to be serious about social mobility, there needs to further support in the form of loans for those on modest incomes to access unpaid internships in certain professions. If this does not materialise then many of the top professions will continue to be a closed shop to most aspiring young people.

2017 General Election and Education

I have mentioned many Conservative achievements in education policy throughout the last seven years. From the Pupil Premium to free childcare, from reforming school structures to more disadvantaged young people going to university than ever before, most major policies have been successful. Nonetheless, when it comes to higher education we have turned students into consumers. Similarly, they are

41 Social Mobility Commission, *State of the Nation 2016: Social Mobility in Great Britain*, 16th November 2016.

consumers when it comes to politics and the 2017 General Election saw a huge increase of 18–24 year olds turning out to vote.

In 2015, 43% of 18–24 year olds voted, this was closer to 70% at the 2017 General Election. This is fantastic for our democracy and helps encourage young people to join the national debate. Regrettably they didn't think the Conservatives were worth voting for even though we introduced free schools, the Pupil Premium and free childcare. Estimations have shown that less than 20% of young people voted Conservatives while 66% voted Labour in 2017. There is no doubt education policy was much to blame for this and if we ignore their concerns then this will be an existential crisis for the Conservatives.

Jeremy Corbyn offered two policies on education that the Conservatives should consider adopting. First, is reintroducing the Education Maintenance Allowance (EMA) for low and middle income 16–18 years when they stay on at school. I received this support myself and it undoubtedly helps many of the poorest young people with travel and lunch expenses. We should promise to bring this back, even if it's just for those whose families earn under £20,000.

Secondly, the Conservatives should seriously consider removing foreign students from the immigration figures. For me this is a no brainer, especially in a post-Brexit world. We should always want the best and the brightest from oversees coming to work in Britain. I'm a firm believer in lowering immigration and cutting the amount of low-skilled immigrants entering the country. But when I discuss this with like-minded people, they have no problem with educated students coming to our country, paying their taxes, supporting our economy and committing virtually no crime.

Obviously the main education policy from Labour at the 2017 General Election (and most expensive) was the £11 billion per year Corbyn promised students through scrapping tuition fees. In addition to this was his £200 billion pledge 'to deal with existing student debt'. During the campaign the Conservatives should have taken this policy apart in so many ways. First, if Labour is going to help the poorest people in society as they claim, why is their biggest funding commitment effectively a tax cut which overwhelmingly benefits the middle class? Second, the argument that tuition fees deter the poorest students from attending university is false. As already stated a poor young person in England is twice as likely to attend university than the tuition fee free zone of Scotland. Third, Labour's policy of abolishing fees would lead to the capping of student numbers and would be financially unsustainable. Where would the money come from if they couldn't raise the money in corporation tax to pay for this spending commitment, which would almost certainly be the case?

The Conservatives should continue to argue that with so many students now attending university, they should pay something towards it, as on average they earn tens of thousands more throughout their career than those who don't go to university. What is progressive about expecting those who don't go to university to pay for somebody who did when they will earn less money?

Even though I have described many arguments in favour of the current system, it is clear that many students are instinctively against the large amount of debt that tuition fees carry. When fees were trebled in 2012, the free market was meant to kick-in and competition for fees would arise. This has not materialised as nearly every university charges the maximum fees, whether it's Sheffield Hallam or Oxford. I propose phasing out tuition fees and shifting to a graduate tax. There would be no debt needed to be paid back (which is the main issue for students) and it can be structured to be highly progressive. If it was introduced at 7% on any earnings over £27,000 it would be a clear indicator that a graduate would have to be on the average UK wage to begin paying back. It would be made affordable by graduates earning over £75,000 paying 10% of their earnings for their university education. But at the same time if they slipped below the £27,000 threshold, nothing would be paid back. With the current tuition fees repayment rate of 9% of earnings over the newly announced threshold of £25,000, this being cut to 7% on earnings up to £75,000 would be a progressive move. The Conservatives need to show that we are listening to young people but we can still make the argument that graduates should pay something back to keep higher education affordable and protect those who didn't go to university from paying more tax.

4 Family & Community

"There's something special about marriage...When you stand up there, in front of your friends and your family, in front of the world, whether it's in a church or anywhere else, what you're doing really means something. And by the way, it means something whether you're a man and a woman, a woman and a woman or a man and another man."[42]

– *David Cameron, 2006*

Introduction

A strong family unit within a cohesive community is essential to any Conservative ideology. For too long we have been defined as slaves to individualism with no regard for society as a collective whole. Margaret Thatcher was famously taken out of context when she said "There is no such thing as society, only individuals and families". This was taken by her enemies as Thatcher showing her true feelings towards society. Namely rugged individualism and an 'in it for yourself' sort of society; not a society built for the common good. Mass unemployment in the 1980s and the public's perception of the Conservatives believing that 'unemployment was a price worth paying' did further damage to the Party.

42 Ibid 5.

David Cameron sought to change the public's attitude to how they saw the Conservative Party's views on society. When elected in December 2005 he stated "There is such thing as society it's just not the same thing as the State".[43] This showed a clear belief in a form of collectivism, but in terms of society not the State. This is an important statement as many who valued families and communities would now give the Conservatives more of a sympathetic hearing. During Cameron's premiership, family and community was a clear priority and it was often at the top of the agenda, even if sometimes controversially. I intend to examine the Conservatives record in promoting family and community, through the lens of social justice and compassionate Conservatism. I have chosen issues as diverse as the Big Society agenda, to same-sex marriage, to immigration's effect on community cohesion.

Several of my previous jobs have helped me develop my thinking on the importance of a strong two-parent family when raising children. Working as a support worker in an inner city homeless hostel, I was left in no doubt the reason for nearly all homelessness. Family breakdown is a scourge in many of our communities and it is a major reason for young people being born into disadvantage where their life chances will never be equal to others. Working in an environment like that I often worried about the life chances of many children being born today. Throughout this chapter I will reference stories from this job and others, in order to show anecdotal evidence for why I believe what I believe. Anybody who seeks a genuinely more meritocratic society surely has to address the causes of family breakdown and how we can lessen its impact.

I do not intend to lecture or demonise certain types of people in society; I've already stated my mother was the sole breadwinner in my upbringing. My beliefs are a mixture of

43 Ibid 14.

traditionalist views with a modern edge to them. I do however intend to critique the Left's viewpoint on family in regards to their constant insistence that it is for the State to take control of families lives. What we need is a revolution in responsibility across our country, whether it is in relation to 14-year-old girls getting pregnant or drug addicts becoming homeless because they choose to buy heroin instead of paying the rent.

Analysis since 2010: Introducing the Big Society

In opposition years, David Cameron stated several times that parts of our society was broken. In an era of apparently strong economic growth, societal problems were the key political talking points. With the work of his eccentric adviser Steve Hilton, the antidote to these social ills was the Big Society initiative. Even though this was the main vision set by the leadership, there is no doubt that The Big Society failed to capture the public and dare I say the Conservative Party's imagination. This further became the case after the global economic meltdown occurred in 2008 as priorities shifted to the economy.

Although the Big Society is a much mocked idea of Cameron's, I must admit I am more than sympathetic to it. It may have been seen as irrelevant when dealing with the budget deficit but it undoubtedly showed the Conservative Party were once again interested in the communities where people live. The Big Society was defined largely into three categories: devolution, social action and the outsourcing of public services. When it comes to increasing the life chances of the most disadvantaged, it is social action which is most pertinent and this is what I will focus on. The idea that people do more for their families and their communities has taken hold in recent years in a variety of successful policies.

The free schools programme is one such policy initiative. As stated in the previous chapter, this is where parents, teachers and charities can set up their own schools, free from local authority control. Many of the merits have already been described but there is no doubt, communities being able to set up their own schools for their children is a huge part of the Big Society. Another achievement in relation to the Big Society was the creation of the National Citizen Service (NCS). This is where 15–17 year olds attend a residential to learn team skills, employability, life skills and work together on a social action project. Thousands of young people have taken part in this and it has changed the lives of many. I once worked on an NCS project, teaching employability skills to one of the groups and it was fantastic seeing so many enthusiastic and motivated young people from all different backgrounds learning from each other.

I may have been one of a small group but the Big Society genuinely captured my imagination. Social action in particular has always been a huge interest of mine. When I was 16, I participated in a cross-community youth group back in Northern Ireland, we sought to learn more about the Protestant and Catholic identities from the others perspective. In 2011 whilst attending university in Sheffield, I volunteered for a year helping primary school children with their homework. This was often quite a difficult challenge as they were mainly from a Somalian background and many struggled with reading and writing in English. In 2012–13 I volunteered with the homelessness and housing charity, Shelter. This was a fantastic experience as I was given the opportunity to shadow support workers and understand the actions which were put in place in ensuring people would not become homeless in the first place. The volunteering experiences I had at university chimed with the social action the Coalition Government were encouraging. If more people had bought into the narrative of the Big Society, this could have been a great success.

2011 Riots

The reason I began to volunteer at the homework club in 2011 was in direct response to the previous summer's riots.

I realised there was deep isolation and lack of community in many of our great cities. If children are living in the United Kingdom with parents who do not speak English, this has a detrimental impact on their life chances. A meritocratic society should be open to all in this country, whether they are born here or have chosen to settle here from elsewhere in the world. My personal response to the riots was in accordance with what David Cameron was saying.

From what started as demonstrators being concerned over a policeman shooting Mark Duggan in London, it turned into a full blown assault on this country. In August 2011 shops were looted, several people were killed and livelihoods were destroyed. The disgusting greed and materialism of the rioters showed a deep moral breakdown in some of our communities. Instead of peacefully protesting about a perceived injustice against the police, the majority were more concerned with stocking up on plasma TVs and trainers.

Duggan's death was an irrelevance to the vast majority of the looters. By the end of it five people were killed, 299 police officers injured and about 2,500 shops and businesses were destroyed. It took the heroic intervention of a grieving father Tariq Jahan, to capture the mood of the nation and call for unity in the community. This horrendous summer further strengthened my belief in the importance of family values with social responsibility.

Reactions to the riots between the Left and the Right of the political spectrum are fundamental examples of why I am a Conservative. Ken Livingstone blamed the public spending squeeze for the actions of people smashing up shops and destroying people's livelihoods, although the cuts had barely begun at this point. Seamus Milne, a genuine Marxist with sympathies for the old Soviet Union (now Jeremy Corbyn's Communication's Director) wrote in the *Guardian* it was David Cameron's fault for the riots as they copied his selfish behaviour! Having just typed their views, I feel extremely angry that's actually what they believed at the time.

The Conservatives on the other hand blamed immoral behaviour from many young people because this is what they have been taught was acceptable. The riots occurred because of total disregard for family, community and social responsibility. This 'me first, take what you can' culture needed to be tackled head on. With not enough being done to help the most problematic families in society know the difference between right and wrong, The Troubled Families Programme[44] was developed as a policy response in December 2011.

This is one of the Coalition Government's most notable policy implementations to reduce inequality and promote social justice. With the government attempting to deal with the budget deficit, this programme was to deal with the responsibility deficit.

David Cameron announced that 120,000 families had cost the taxpayer £9 billion in the preceding year. Each of these families would have a named 'family worker'. There were three main aims which would measure the success of the programme. First, those in the family who could work should be employed or be on their way into employment. Second, children should always attend school and truancy should be curbed. Third, no member of the family should be in trouble with the law for at least six months. This holistic approach by the government was to give the youngest members of each family more support and better opportunities than their parents had.

Was the Troubled Families Programme a success? The government claimed to have a 99% success rate with the 120,000 families which were helped.[45] There was also the claim that this saved the taxpayers £1.2 billion by changed

44 http://researchbriefings.parliament.uk/ResearchBriefing/Summary/CBP-7585 [Accessed 6th May 2017]

45 https://www.theguardian.com/society/2015/nov/11/troubled-family-programme-government-success-council-figures [Accessed 6th May 2017]

behaviours. This confidence in the programme led to its massive expansion to 400,000 families by 2020 but councils would only be paid if families were successful. This payment by results has undoubtedly led to councils claiming short-term success as they sought payments.

Short-term outcomes are a poor measure as many of these families have clear long-term social problems. Some believed that the government underestimated the scale of the difficulties faced by the most entrenched families and overestimated the scheme to transform the lives of those who participated. The Troubled Families Programme was invariably a great initiative and should not be disbanded but extended. The May Government has recognised this and reforms have put into motion which will be discussed later in this chapter.

Marriage

In the Coalition years the Conservative Party had a trickier relationship with marriage than many expected. Conservatives nearly always support the institution of marriage and David Cameron was no exception. However, marriage meant something different to Cameron than it did to about half of the Conservative membership. As far back as 2006 Cameron made a case for spreading marriage at the Conservative Conference, stating "It means something whether you're a man and a woman, a woman and a woman or a man and another man".[46]

In his 2011 party conference speech Cameron proclaimed "I don't support same-sex marriage despite being a Conservative, I support gay marriage because I am a Conservative".[47] Cameron believed marriage increased social mobility and sought to spread the institution. Many Conservative activists disagreed with this view and at this

46 Ibid 5.

47 David Cameron, Conservative Party Conference, 4th October 2011.

point, a significant number left the party to join UKIP. When same-sex marriage was enacted it was a great triumph for Cameron as a statesman but left him weakened within the Conservative Party. Traditionalist Conservatives and more liberally minded Conservatives split on this issue more than any other since the Conservative Party re-entered government in 2010. Luckily the split has not been terminal since same-sex marriage was implemented.

Although many in the Conservative Party disagreed with Cameron over same-sex marriage, there was more agreement on recognising marriage as part of the tax system. This was announced in 2013 after a transactional deal was completed with the Liberal Democrats for them to abstain in a vote. The marriage tax allowance lets one half of a married couple transfer part of their tax-free allowance to their partner. Cameron didn't expect this to mean that couples would be flocking to the nearest church or registry office to get married to claim this, he simply wanted to give a signal that the government was on the side of married couples. With there being over 4 million married couples and those in civil partnerships benefiting from this tax incentive, this provides a little extra income to married couples in supporting their children and ultimately improve their life chances.

Immigration

Some may wonder why I have included the topic of immigration in the family and community chapter. This is because many people have seen their communities change out of all recognition in the last decade and the Conservatives attempted to rectify this when in government by reducing immigration.

It's important to remember that when Britain was the 'sick man of Europe' in the 1970s, we had the problem of more people leaving Britain than entering the country. This led to a shortage of skilled workers and an older population rapidly increasing. By the 1990s under John Major's Government, net migration (the difference of people entering the country to the people who are leaving) was roughly about 50,000. Many saw this level as manageable and the great British public did not see immigration as an issue. Events of 2004 changed everything with the policy of the Blair Government that removed transitional controls to Eastern European countries such as Poland and Lithuania. The government predicted that 13,000 extra migrants would come to Britain in the first few years but over 1 million arrived instead. Net migration under Labour peaked at nearly 300,000 in 2006 and public concern about changing communities grew massively thereafter.

David Cameron pledged at the 2010 General Election that immigration would be controlled and net migration would fall to under 100,000 under the Conservatives. This has arguably been the Conservative's greatest failure in government. Despite closing down bogus colleges and restricting access for many potential newcomers from outside the European Union, net migration has continued at record levels.

This manifesto pledge was misguided at best as the government had no restrictions on the free movement of people from within the EU. The failure to control immigration has had a detrimental impact and contributed to the lowest paid people in Britain not seeing a pay rise throughout these years. The minimum wage became the maximum wage as anybody with even a basic understanding of economics would appreciate that an oversupply of low-skilled labour keeps down wages. With the June 2016 vote to leave the EU, new steps should be taken to control immigration and these will be discussed later in this chapter.

Conservative Values in Modern Britain

Beliefs and values of the traditional conservative family unit were undoubtedly challenged by Cameron's more liberal-minded Conservatism. There may be somewhat of a generational or cultural divide but both sides of the Conservative coin recognise that a strong family is vital when improving social mobility. With cutting the budget deficit being the overarching priority of the Coalition Government, the Conservatives promoting the family took a back seat in many ways. The most notable change which took place was ultimately same-sex marriage. This upset the Conservative base enormously and was seen as an irrelevance by many in promoting social mobility through a strong family unit.

The marriage tax allowance appeased some on the Conservative backbenches but many would have liked to see more of a focus on tackling family breakdown and promoting life chances for all. I intend to do this with my own ideas later on in this chapter.

Cameron clearly wished to have more of an impact on promoting strong communities than his Conservative predecessors. With the emphasis on the Big Society and devolving more power to local communities, there were some successes. Although the riots happened on the Conservatives watch, they showed us all that much more help needs to be given to the poorest communities so we can improve the life chances of the many.

The Coalition Government and the Conservative majority government's failure on immigration led to many of the lowest paid workers' wages being squeezed and many communities feeling overwhelmed by mass immigration. As we enter the next parliament, a clear plan needs to be created to strengthen social responsibility in our society and to encourage a shared British identity which all can adhere to.

Moving Forward: Strengthening Family and Community

For me, David Cameron's best speech as party leader was at the 2015 Conservative Conference. He outlined and defined many causes and issues in relation to family breakdown in Britain today. He promised an "all-out assault on poverty".[48] He identified the problems of "Homes where no-one works; children growing up in chaos; addiction, mental health problems, abuse, family breakdown". Some of the facts that Cameron shared during that speech scared but didn't surprise me. He stated that a teenager is more likely to own a smartphone than have a dad living with them. Every day in Britain three babies are born addicted to heroin. Seventy percent of prostitutes were once in care. Care leavers are four times more likely to commit suicide than anyone else. David Cameron identified many of the problems arising with family breakdown but new policy initiatives after the 2015 General Election were not forthcoming as the EU referendum took centre stage.

With Theresa May not wishing to let Brexit totally dominate the political agenda, Cameron's vision of an 'all-out assault on poverty' should be promoted by the Conservatives. In promoting this assault on poverty, tackling family breakdown and building strong communities is crucial to building a socially just meritocratic country.

Tackling Family Breakdown

A long term way to cut public spending is to tackle the causes of family breakdown. This costs tens of billions of pounds a year to the taxpayer. Parenting has a bigger influence on a child's outcomes than any other factor. Working in a homeless hostel I saw the massive cost to the taxpayer of family breakdown. Whether it was the cost of Housing Benefit from those who lived there, to the cost to the NHS due to teenage

48 David Cameron, Conservative Party Conference, 7th October 2015.

pregnancies, mental health conditions and drug and alcohol addictions, never mind the massive costs to police budgets dealing with crime.

Even in-work benefits are usually claimed because of family breakdown. My mother claimed Child Tax Credit because there was no other earner in the home. If there are two parents working full-time they will almost certainly not be claiming in-work benefits. When families do separate, there is the terrible issue of unpaid child maintenance. In 2017, the BBC reported that there was £3.8 billion worth of backlog in unpaid child maintenance.[49]

Extending the Troubled Families Programme is crucial in the 'all-out assault on poverty'. We genuinely need a revolution in responsibility. During my time as a support worker in the homeless hostel, it never ceased to amaze me the attitude of some young girls who were pregnant with their third child to the third different dad, who expected me to congratulate them on the fact they were pregnant with another child they could not look after. Or the many drug addicts who simply refused to pay any rent as heroin would always be their only priority.

We need to encourage couples to stay together as children of two-parent families generally have better life outcomes, in terms of education and income, in large part because they have more resources available. We also need to support our young people in care by prioritising their education when moved out of their family home, not just throwing money at them for materialistic purposes. We need to drastically cut reoffending rates by giving them a way out of crime. Extra support is needed for initiatives such as helping troubled young people join the army and further increased access to apprenticeships.

Training programmes, employment support and drug and alcohol support is the way to strengthen the Troubled

49 http://www.bbc.co.uk/news/uk-39293209 [Accessed 14th May 2017]

Families Programme. The biggest disincentive to supporting our most disadvantaged people is to make the welfare state more generous. As I will show in the next chapter, excessive welfare payments are the enemy to social mobility as it encourages people to stay where they are and not stand on their own two feet.

Further Ideas for Unleashing Community Engagement

As well as the importance of confronting family breakdown, a new strategy for building stronger communities needs to be created. Dare I say we need a return to the Big Society theme? To fund this, I feel we can return to Big Lottery Funding. Currently, every £2 spent on a Lottery ticket, 56 pence (28%) goes to 'good causes'. Billions have been raised since its inception in 2004 and community organisations see the vast majority of this funding. If the percentage of the Lottery tickets that went to charity, went up from 28% to say, 40%, millions more a year would be raised for charitable causes. This could lead to many new projects which aim to build cohesive communities.

One example could be a project to increase volunteering amongst students. When I was at university I was taken aback by the amount of students who had no contact with the average person living in Sheffield and I thought it was a shame. If volunteering could be encouraged much more at universities, students would benefit from learning about the wider society they live in. Whether it be teaching ICT to the elderly or helping job seekers with English and Maths, if more students could offer their services to wider society, everyone would benefit. When I volunteered at the homework club or with Shelter, I learnt a lot more about the community I lived in.

Local government and devolution deals are another key way of building strong communities and helping the poorest progress. I know from experience that local authorities have lost too much of their budgets and there needs to be a small increase again to support the local services such as homelessness and social care. No doubt back in 2010 efficiency savings were needed and the pay of chief executives was and is still shocking. There should be a cap on local authority chief executives pay as in dozens of cases they are on six figure salaries. This money should be put back into the frontline.

Local authorities need to have the money to pay for adult social care, children in care and the homeless. With central government grants being phased out and local authorities being allowed to keep all their business rates, devolution deals will be vital for attracting extra investment to local communities. Local Enterprise Partnerships have been a great initiative. This is where councils and local business leaders work together to bring investment to the area thus tackling unemployment in local areas. Every Local Enterprise Partnership and local authority should be working together to expand private sector jobs and bring down youth unemployment. This expansion of local jobs will be imperative in strengthening many run down communities.

Immigration Reform

To further support our communities, we need to reduce immigration and instead focus on integration. David Cameron's failed targets of less than 100,000 should still be our goal as we will never be able to promote integration if we continue to allow 600,000 people a year coming in and therefore living in segregated communities. Before the howling Left seek to attack me, I think immigration is fantastic. Immigrants make our communities more diverse and they make Britain what it is today. I am massively pro-immigration but that does not mean I am pro-mass immigration.

When I first moved to Sheffield in 2010 and worked in McDonald's, I loved working with so many people from different countries. They were hard working, generous and friendly. Yet I did often think to myself, with nearly 1 million British young people out of work, don't they deserve more of a chance? The general retort to this is that British people are lazy and dismissive of jobs like McDonald's. If this is the case (which on the whole, I don't think it is) that's why welfare reforms have been brought in since 2010.

When I was living in Sheffield I got speaking to a teacher one evening. She told me she loved her job, the children she taught and that she was an open-minded liberal who loved diversity. Then she went on to say that there were 50 languages spoken in her school and therefore she couldn't do her job properly. As she had to focus her efforts on the children who could barely speak English, the rest were ultimately somewhat neglected. With my limited experience of helping migrant children with their homework, I had great sympathy but couldn't begin to comprehend how difficult her job must be. She went on to tell me that she was going to vote UKIP in the future because she believed that immigration should be controlled. The teacher said she felt terrible for it but she had to think with her head, not her heart.

How can we build integrated communities when there are good decent teachers like this who feel they have no choice but to vote UKIP? Over half a billion pounds a year is spent on children in our schools whose first language isn't English. In many of our communities, class sizes are far too large and there simply isn't enough school places available for the amount of people living there.

Other public services are under great strain partly due to mass migration. The NHS has more patients than ever before but it has to be said that it would collapse without the support of migrants. That's why in a post-EU Britain we still need to bring in nurses and other healthcare professionals from across the world to work in the NHS. At the same time, we need to train more British people to do these jobs and encourage more people to be carers.

Housing is a different issue entirely. Let's be clear it is the government's fault that we haven't got enough houses, but mass immigration exacerbates the crisis. When I worked in homelessness, speaking to many of the homeless, they were resentful that they would not be allocated a council house but migrants would be because of the way 'need' was assessed. This builds resentment in our communities and this is one of the many reasons why we need to tackle the housing crisis.

Public services need migrants working in them, like the NHS and social care. British people recognise and are grateful for this. At the same time, it is unarguably the case that mass immigration puts huge strains on our schools, housing and waiting times in the NHS. We are already one of the most densely populated countries in Europe therefore more control over our borders needs to be exercised if we are to encourage integration.

Mass immigration leads to negative consequences for the lowest paid wages as well for public services. As I stated at the beginning of this chapter, the minimum wage has become the maximum wage. It has led to wage compression for many low income workers and was a massive factor for many voting Leave in 2016.

If there is an oversupply of low-skilled labour from Eastern Europe available to work in fast food outlets, then what pressure is there for big businesses to give workers a pay rise? For the British self-employed plumber who may have been on £16 an hour, he will be undercut if an Eastern European plumber comes along and says he will do the same job for £12 an hour.

This compression of wages was surely the main reason for Osborne introducing the living wage. When we reach £9 an hour by 2020 we will have one of the highest minimum wages in any developed economy. This will mean we will become even more attractive to low-skilled workers from afar, a major reason why we need to control our borders again. This is nothing to do with where somebody is from or the colour of their skin, like the Left try to make out; it is to do with improving the lot of low and medium earners who live in the United Kingdom.

Let's Reclaim Family and Community

We should all have personal responsibility in society, but additionally we should have social responsibility to one another. This is a clear differentiation between Labour's top-down big State centralising approach and the Thatcherite individualism of the 1980s.

For too long those of us on the common sense centre have not been allowed to say that we believe that the best way of bringing up a child is in a two-parent family. For too long we have let the powerful forces of the State intrude on what should be the responsibilities of parents. For too long we have been called ignorant and racist because we believe that Britain should determine the quality and quantity of people who can enter this country.

What many on the Left don't understand is that family and community cohesion is essential to improving social mobility. Two parents working and living in a decent area are far more likely to have a child who will be successful in life. Consequences of family breakdown, like the suffering of a mental health issue or antisocial behaviour is almost certainly going to have a detrimental impact on children of such families. When it comes to community there is nothing wrong with expecting your child to attend a school where teachers have the resources to focus on the majority of the class. There is nothing wrong with believing that we need to reduce the flow of low-skilled migrants from abroad as workers face endless wage compression as a result of this. As Conservatives we once again need to bang the drum and link strong families and integrated communities together in order to successfully promote meritocracy for all.

5 Welfare & Poverty

"Our real success has been to reframe the argument – challenging a narrative beloved of the Left, which focuses on how much is being spent on welfare that it risks overlooking the real question...that it is not about how much goes into the benefit system, but what difference it makes to people at the other end."[50]

– Iain Duncan Smith, 2014

Introduction

Welfare reform and spending has always been of interest to me because it has been part of my personal and employment background. My mother claimed Working Tax Credits for the vast majority of my childhood as she raised three children in a single income family.

When it comes to my employment history, as a homelessness support worker I saw first-hand how much the poorest people heavily depend on benefit payments. When working in job centres for a charity, I saw the range of efforts from those looking for work in job centres. It's because I've been involved in large parts of this world that I have such strong beliefs in regards to the role of welfare spending and its impact on aspiration and promoting social mobility. Fundamentally I believe that we should support those who are genuinely too

50 Iain Duncan Smith Speech, Centre for Social Justice, 23rd January 2014.

sick to work but for those who can work we should be giving them a 'hand up not a hand out'.

In 2014, as part of a two-day training course on making sure the homeless were in receipt of the correct benefits, I was struck by the change of tone of my left-wing colleagues once they saw the entitlements available. This was even after four years of austerity from a Conservative-led government. As the trainer lambasted the Conservatives welfare reforms, including the £26,000 benefit cap, interestingly I could see that people who I knew to be left-wing didn't agree with him.

As a worker would have to be earning £34,000 to be receiving £26,000 after tax, I can see why there wasn't too much sympathy as support workers in the room like me were earning £15,000 a year. If it is paying to be on welfare rather than be in work, it sends the message that Britain is not in favour of a society where people can get on in life, but a society where we pay certain groups of people good money not to be in work.

Throughout this chapter I will often refer to anecdotal stories from my background, particularly with the homeless. These anecdotal stories will illustrate the government policies in practice since 2010. In previous chapters I have outlined many of the incentives that the government have put in place to encourage individuals into work including tax cuts, the living wage and free childcare. Such incentives show that it pays to be in work and this shift is vital to maintain if we are to increase social mobility.

This will be emphasised throughout as there is no doubt that these policies have softened the financial blow of reduced welfare spending. Although, it must be said that we still have one of the highest proportions of welfare spending in the world. As George Osborne stated in 2015, "We have got 1% of the world's population, 4% of its GDP, but we undertake 7% of the world's welfare spending".[51] This truly

51 George Osborne, PMQ's, 17th June 2015.

is an unsustainable amount and justifies the government's previous reforms and evidently shows we need to undertake further welfare reform. We need a revolution in individual and social responsibility if we are to tackle the dependency culture and help promote upward mobility amongst lower income households.

1997–2010: Record of the Last Labour Government

After ten years of continuous years of economic growth under New Labour between 1997–2007 and with unemployment very low, you would think that welfare spending would have fallen. Unfortunately, the opposite was true. Welfare spending nearly doubled under New Labour as they deliberately sucked more and more people into reliance on state benefits. This came in the form of both out of work benefits and noticeably through in-work benefits.

The former mainly includes Employment and Support Allowance (ESA) and Disability Living Allowance (DLA). The latter mainly includes Working and Child Tax Credits, introduced by Gordon Brown. This spending did not go unnoticed by the general public as Labour was often accused of being the 'party of welfare'. Former Labour leadership candidate, Liz Kendall, in 2015 often referenced people on the doorstop saying they couldn't support Labour as they were in work not on welfare.

While employment grew under Labour, rates of economic inactivity remained extremely high. By 2007, 21% of the workforce was deemed economically inactive. Over 2 million people of working age were on long-term sickness benefits with a significant number aged under 25. By 2010 at the end of Brown's time as prime minister, nearly 5 million people in Britain of working age were on some form of out of work benefit.

The strategy under Labour was to leave these people on sickness benefits and replace them with an unprecedented wave of migrants, mainly low-skilled, who would take the jobs that were being created. Under New Labour, the vast majority of new jobs went to foreign workers. Many traditional Labour supporters had major concerns about this policy and it led to resentment in many working-class communities. Growing up in Northern Ireland I knew dozens of people claiming sickness benefits who were capable of work. Labour did not take this on as an issue due to fear of bad headlines for individual cases.

The introduction of Working Tax Credits was initially seen as a way to 'top-up' the pay of those who are in work but on low pay. Child Tax Credits were introduced for those on low pay or for unemployed parents. This was Labour's idea 'for making working pay'. But instead of this, such Tax Credits have led to perverse incentives. Former Labour Welfare minister, Frank Field, argued at the time that they would penalise families for wanting to work more hours and would also discourage saving. Indeed, people claiming Tax Credits would be penalised for working more hours, being taxed at a rate of 90%. Thus encouraging underemployment.

Instead of introducing free childcare for low income families, they were sucked into welfare dependency. Instead of introducing a real living wage or cutting taxes for the lowest paid, millions of families were encouraged to claim Tax Credits and become reliant on the welfare state. In addition to this, the Tax Credit system incentivised employers to keep wages low as the workers would be perpetually subsidised by the State.

Many on the Left would be outraged by this analysis of welfare and the last Labour Government. They patronisingly think that low income people can't think for themselves and should therefore have no responsibility for anything. If millions of people are on out of work sickness benefits, "It's not their fault; they can't be expected to work as old industries like mining have been destroyed". Of course there are many hardships in Britain because of deindustrialisation but writing people off should never be the choice made by government.

The Left actively seek to build a larger welfare state because this means the individual admits defeat and they must rely on a large state to be responsible for their life. I hope with my personal experiences I can take on this condescending attitude to keeping lower income people in their place and promote positive aspiration instead.

As John Major said when he was growing up on a council estate. "The Labour Party said be patient, stay where you are and in time we will help you; the Conservatives said we will give you the tools to help and improve yourself."[52] Ultimately, as the background of John Major shows, individual endeavour and perseverance is the way to improve yourself.

Reform or Cuts? Welfare and Poverty Since 2010

According to the British Social Attitudes Survey, in 1989 after ten years of tough Thatcherite policies, 61% of the public supported spending more on welfare for the poor. Understandably this may have influenced the incoming Labour Government in 1997 that welfare spending needed to increase. However, by 2009, after 12 years of a Labour Government, only 27% of the public thought that welfare spending should increase.[53] The reasons for this dramatic drop in public support for welfare spending is evidenced in what I've written previously and this drop meant that it was imperative that when the Conservatives entered into government in 2010, welfare was drastically reformed.

As the Coalition Government took office in 2010 with a radical plan to reform welfare there was tension at the top of government. The often demonised Work and Pensions Secretary, Iain Duncan Smith (IDS), spoke about redemption and did not wish to stigmatise those without jobs. His priority was to mainly reform welfare, encourage a change in attitude

52 Ibid 1.

53 http://www.bsa.natcen.ac.uk/latest-report/british-social-attitudes-32/welfare.aspx [Accessed 18th May 2017]

and improve social mobility for families who spent many years in the work wilderness.

On the other hand, with the biggest budget deficit in the Western world, George Osborne was sceptical of reform and sought to save money. He painted a picture to the public of the undeserving shirker and the deserving striver. Although there is no question there was some truth in what he was stating, this tone was unhelpful. Even with the tension of priorities between IDS and Osborne, radical reforms were introduced. Ending the dependency culture whilst promoting work and therefore social mobility was the vision of the Conservatives in government.

Benefit Cap

One of the first big welfare announcements was the introduction of the Benefit Cap at £26,000 a year per family. The idea was that the average family on benefits would not receive more money than the average person's salary. Disability benefits were exempt from this cap and the cap would not have any impact if there was somebody in the family working at least 16 hours a week.

According to government figures this encouraged at least 12,000 more people in less than year get a job before the cap was introduced in 2013. The Left's outcry at this policy looked ridiculous as opinions polls have shown that 73% of the public supported it. The vast majority actually thought that the cap should be set at a lower level. This was duly introduced by the Conservatives in 2016 who brought the cap down to £20,000 outside London and £23,000 in London. To receive £20,000 in a salary would require a gross salary of over £24,000. The public once again saw this policy as fair and just, so unlimited payments of benefits did not result in unlimited lack of aspiration, which in turn is the enemy of social mobility.

Contrarily, Jeremy Corbyn has vowed to scrap the cap ever since he was elected as leader of the Labour Party in 2015. The benefit cap has not saved much money in the welfare budget but it is seen as a symbolic gesture that there should be limits to benefit entitlements.

Disability Benefits

In 1992, 1.1 million people claimed Disability Living Allowance (DLA), by 2013 it was 3.3 million. This threefold rise in disability claimants is an extraordinary statistic which led the government to propose reform to the benefit. That was the original idea when the government moved from DLA to Personal Independence Payment (PIP). The vast majority of people on DLA were never reassessed and left on the benefit indefinitely. PIP actually offered higher benefit payments to those deemed most in need.

George Osborne obviously thought the payment was too high as he proposed a substantial cut to PIP, prompting the inevitable resignation of IDS in 2016. As this cut would have effected those already claiming the benefit, this brewed trouble within the Conservative ranks. For many this was a welfare cut too far and Osborne abandoned this before the Conservative backbenchers voted it down.

Hand in hand with DLA reform was the use of Work Capability Assessments for those claiming Employment and Support Allowance (first brought in under Labour in 2007). This was to distinguish between those who had a medical condition so severe they were unable to work (the Support Group) and those who with the appropriate support could return to the labour market (the Work Related Group). These assessments, which have been contracted to Atos and Capita have proved somewhat controversial. A large number of successful appeals have been lodged against the Work Capability Assessments. Since April 2017, new Work Related ESA claimant's benefits will be paid the same amount as those on Job Seeker's Allowance (JSA). To improve the chances of these people being encouraged to find work I will explain later on this chapter why I think this change is important.

As I've already indicated, although the majority of people who claim disability benefits clearly need them, my personal and employment experiences have led me to believe that there are a lot of people who are wrongly claiming these benefits. For example, during my time as a homelessness support worker I couldn't believe the number of drug addicts who were able to claim DLA or PIP because they had given themselves a disability by injecting drugs. If they had injected themselves in the groin (which most heroin addicts I came across did), they could claim both care and mobility components for disability benefits as this effected their movement and ability to look after themselves.

PIP/DLA, ESA and Housing Benefit quite often led to them being able to claim more than £1,500 a month in benefits (much more than the £1,100 I was earning after tax as their support worker). One heroin addict was claiming £1,500 a month in benefits and yet he used the quilts from the hostel to sit in Nottingham City Centre and beg on the streets. He would often boast when he returned to the hostel that he could earn £200 a day from the general public, on top of his benefit payments. I often wondered how we could progress as a society when we subsidise and therefore encourage people's addictions. The cleaner in the homeless hostel earned £6.50 an hour to clean up the dirty needles left behind by many of the addicts who were receiving much more money. From the residents living in the homeless hostel, a major issue I came across was those who were in the ESA Work Related Group who should clearly have been claiming JSA. There were a variety of reasons for this but two main reasons came up time and time again.

First, was that those on ESA have much less pressure to look for work than those on JSA. Secondly, was the fact that if you claim Work Related ESA then you were entitled to £30 a week more than somebody on JSA. Sadly, I came across more than a handful of people who would openly say to me and indeed encourage to others 'to play on your mental health' so they would be put on ESA instead of JSA. This is the definition of a poverty of aspiration and thinking back I am even more disenchanted that nearly all people who said this were young.

Tragically, out of the near 400 residents I came across in the hostel, far too many were young. Many had come from families where nobody worked and the eagerness to want to claim disability benefits was soul destroying. From one 16-year-old demanding a DLA form because he had ADHD, to another one who refused to look for work and claimed for ESA because he bruised his finger, it was an indictment on our society. There is no doubt that because of welfare reform many people have wrongly had benefits withdrawn but from my experience there are just as many who seek to fund their lifestyle via the taxpayer.

Tougher Conditions for JSA Claimants

Job seekers faced tougher rules under the Conservatives with the amount of hours they had to spend looking for work. If several interviews were not attended at the jobcentre or a job not accepted, then they would be sanctioned. This tough policy was introduced to embolden job seekers to take more responsibility in finding a job.

In 2011, the Work Programme was introduced by the Conservative-led Coalition, replacing Labour's welfare to work schemes. This was to help the long-term unemployed (over 9 months) to find work. This was contracted out to private, public and charitable providers on a payment by results basis. A study in 2014 showed that only 27% of those who entered onto the Work Programme had kept sustainable employment after six months.[54] This is a low figure but is still

54 National Audit Office, 2014b.

27% more with a pay packet than before the programme was launched.

One of the other schemes introduced by the Coalition Government was the Work Experience Programme. This involved companies providing a voluntary unpaid work placement of between two to eight weeks, but participants would continue to receive JSA. This work experience would have been a positive addition to a person's CV as it would've shown the correct attitude for when they eventually entered the job market. In 2013, programmes like this soon became irrelevant as the economy picked up and many new jobs were created. Unemployment peeked at 8.5% in 2011 (still extremely low by EU standards) but had fallen to 4.3% by late 2017.

Back in 2009, I remember attending the Job Centre in Northern Ireland with a friend I grew up with who was signing on. We walked into the centre and he went over to the nearest computer and printed off five random job applications. He then went over to an advisor with 'proof' he had been looking for work. There appeared to be no issue and therefore no problem with claiming his benefits. He had no intention in looking for a job and I couldn't believe how easy it was.

This sort of attitude is why the Conservatives created the Work Programme and expanded benefit sanctions. I remember when working in 2011 at McDonald's in Sheffield, the Socialist Workers Party were outside protesting with placards saying we were hiring 'slave labour' and nobody was actually being offered jobs. The opposite was true as in the McDonald's I worked in, the vast majority of those who attended the Work Experience Scheme were offered jobs at the end of it.

When working in job centres, I would help individuals with writing CVs, cover letters and interview skills. Unfortunately, several of the JSA claimants were not happy to receive this extra support. During this time, I helped several dozen young people into work. This experience made me realise that tougher conditions must be put into place so that those out of work are not allowed to fester on benefits but instead should be aspiring to get a job as soon as possible.

Tax Credits and Child Benefit

I have already stated my opinion that instead of introducing Tax Credits, New Labour should have created a living wage and raised the personal tax allowance. When Tax Credits were introduced they cost several billion but over the years this has ballooned to over £40 billion. Those claiming Tax Credits faced a disincentive to work as there was a marginal tax rate of anywhere between 60%-90%. This meant that many people were kept underemployed and it didn't pay to work. This has been partly addressed by Universal Credit which will be discussed later in this chapter.

Since the Conservatives have taken office, middle earners have been restricted from claiming Child Tax Credits and higher earners Child Benefit (as discussed in previous chapters). With income tax cuts compensating for these benefit withdrawals, the Conservatives have sought to create a low tax and low welfare society, instead of a high tax high welfare society. Furthermore, it was announced by George Osborne in 2014 that all working age benefits would be frozen until 2020, this includes Tax Credits and Child Benefit.

In recent years' Tax Credits have risen up the political agenda resulting in much controversy. In the 2015 Emergency Budget, George Osborne proposed that out of £12 billion worth of welfare cuts, £4.5 billion would be from Tax Credits. This would have effectively increased the marginal tax rate of those who wanted to work more and many claimants would have faced a cut in payments of up to £3,000 per year.

Although the living wage and further tax cuts were to be introduced, this would not be enough to compensate. After much opposition by the media, opposition parties,

Conservative backbenchers and the House of Lords, the cuts were eventually dropped. This was possibly the lowest moment during Osborne's Chancellorship as the speed of the cuts meant that it was impossible to argue that he was in anyway helping the lowest earners.

Another major announcement made by Osborne was the limiting of Child Tax Credits to the first two children from April 2017. There is a much stronger case for this policy, as a couple with two incomes of say £19,000 each, couldn't afford to have as many children as they like, why should they be paying for others to have more children? This goes to the heart of the argument about who should be providing for your children, you or the State?

As I've already mentioned, my mother claimed Working and Child Tax Credits for me and my two siblings. They helped a great deal but they were increased far too dramatically at election times by Gordon Brown and too many middle income earners were encouraged to claim support from the State.

Although I was against the cuts in Tax Credits proposed by Osborne in 2015, over the long term they should become less relevant as income tax is cut and the living wage is increased. When working in youth unemployment, I was earning £19,000 a year, after tax about £1,330 a month. I had a friend at the time who was working 16 hours a week at McDonald's, earning about £500 a month. They had one child and was a single income household, but the State was supplementing this £500 income with another £1,300 a month. Somebody working 16 hours a week getting about two thirds of the hourly rate I was receiving, came out with nearly £500 more a month than I received. This took the shape of Housing Benefit, Child Benefit and Council Tax Discount but the main payment was Tax Credits, which made up the vast majority of this top-up.

This person found that if they worked more hours at McDonald's they would lose money and it was financially better to work just 16 hours a week. If Tax Credits were allowed to stay as they were this would consign millions of people to being trapped on perpetual low pay.

Housing Benefit

The Coalition Government faced an ever-rising Housing Benefit bill upon taking office in 2010. With the building of houses declining dramatically after the crash of 2008, wages falling and incomes being squeezed, this was inevitable. In 2008 Housing Benefit cost the taxpayer just over £16 billion a year, by the time the Coalition entered government it had reached over £20 billion. As with other benefits, cuts were needed to be made to slow this growth. The difficulty was that over 5 million people were claiming Housing Benefit in the UK, many of which were in work and on low pay. In 2009–10, 478,000 people with jobs claimed Housing Benefit but by 2017 this rose to over 1 million. This rise in Housing Benefit under the Conservatives shows that house building has remained too low and wages have not risen as highly as expected.

The Housing Benefit Bill has now reached £25 billion a year and is becoming an increasingly higher proportion of the welfare budget. Ninety-five percent of taxpayer spending on housing is going towards Housing Benefit, rather than building houses. Over £9 billion is going to subsidise private landlords – imagine what could be done if we used this money to build more homes?

One of, if not the most controversial policy brought in by the Conservatives since 2010, has been the removal of the spare room subsidy, or the Bedroom Tax to critics. Aimed to bring down the Housing Benefit bill, claimants deemed to be under-occupying a spare room would have Housing Benefit removed for each spare room they had. This left tenants with the unenviable task of making up the shortfall or downsizing their house.

The idea of downsizing and moving to a smaller home sounds good in theory but in reality there were not enough houses to downsize too. Therefore, many tenants were stuck in their current home with less income to pay for it. This policy would be reasonable if there was not a housing crisis, but due to the current shortage it has caused hardship to many disadvantaged people and should be abandoned.

Universal Credit

The flagship welfare reform under the Conservatives was developed by Iain Duncan Smith and the Centre for Social Justice, before the Coalition was created. The idea was to create a simpler form of financial support for working age adults in low paid work. Universal Credit (UC) has been designed to reduce benefit dependency by providing targeted support for unemployed adults as well as extra financial assistance for low-paid workers.

UC is in the process of replacing existing benefits such as Income Support, Income based JSA, Income related ESA, Housing Benefit, Child and Working Tax Credits. There has been broad cross-party support to simplify the system but UC has faced major criticisms. The online application process has proved difficult for many claimants, monthly instead of by-weekly payments have been criticised and so has the withdrawal of paying rent straight to the landlord. These changes have been made so that the claimant takes more responsibility when claiming benefits and will learn how to improve their budgeting skills. The Conservatives believe this insistence of treating UC like a monthly pay packet will encourage more to feel confident in entering the workplace.

Universal Credit was due to be completely rolled out by 2017 but because of IT problems, costs have spiralled out of control. This means that it is due to be completely rolled out by 2022, a full five-year delay. One of the ways that UC was to be successful was to make work pay. With Iain Duncan

Smith wanting the work allowance to be higher so it 'paid to work', Osborne constantly battled with him to keep the cost of UC down.

In 2015 Osborne eventually won this battle, successfully introducing cuts to UC which would save billions in the long term. The cuts to the work allowance were similar to the proposed cuts to Tax Credits but the crucial difference is that these cuts would be further down the line. By the time the majority of families would be claiming UC, it was argued at the time they would be better off because of the living wage, tax free allowance rise and 30 hours' free childcare. However, if UC is going to truly make work pay, the cuts to the work allowance should be reversed.

Poverty

Before discussing the Conservative record on poverty, I will seek to analyse the definition of poverty in the UK. What academics and left-wing students do not understand is that when the average person in Britain thinks about poverty, they think of the developing world. They think of children not being able to have access to clean water, shelter or an education. It is a fearful heart-wrenching word which should not be taken lightly.

The way poverty is measured in the UK is unjustifiable. If somebody earns less than 60% of the median income, then by British standards, they are in relative poverty. By definition this means there will always be millions of people in 'poverty' in Britain. It means that I have spent the majority of my life in 'poverty', from when I was growing up to when I was working as a homelessness support worker. This is despite the fact that I had access to three meals a day and I certainly was not in poverty.

Alongside the majority of the population, when I hear Labour politicians like Jeremy Corbyn stating there is greater poverty in Britain than ever before, I think it's a shameful use of language. Especially if you know even the most basic history about children working down chimneys and poor people being sent to the workhouse in the nineteenth century. Iain Duncan Smith did try to change the poverty definition so it would bring in other factors but this was vetoed by Osborne because of the potential financial implications.

Upon the Conservatives entering government in 2010, there were fears that austerity cuts would mean poverty dramatically increasing as benefits were withdrawn. David Cameron sought to pivot the government away from income poverty and look at the underlying causes of deprivation such as family breakdown and poor schooling. This objective has proven successful as there is now the lowest level of worklessness households on record.

However, there have been major issues over the use of food banks since the Conservatives introduced austerity measures. This may be a phenomenon in the Western world but food banks have been on the increase during the last decade. Many on the Left claim this is because of benefit sanctions and many in the Conservative Party have claimed this is because they are now advertised in job centres. By 2015 over 1 million food packages were given out by food banks up and down the country. This is undoubtedly a large increase in the last decade but these statistics were deliberately misrepresented by the Labour Party. They have constantly claimed over 1 million people a year are using food banks but what is recorded is that 1 million packages were given out. As the majority of people using food banks return to them regularly, I estimate that less than a half a million people a year are actually using food banks.

When working with the homeless, I often visited food banks with residents who lived in the hostel. When Theresa May stated that there were complex reasons as to why people visited food banks, the Left scorned her response. But she was undoubtedly right. I referred and took residents to food banks many times and for a variety of reasons. Some were because they had been sanctioned by the job centre, many because of refusal to fulfil their contract of looking for a job. Others were because they had just put in a new claim because they had recently been released from prison or hospital. A frequent reason was that they were under 18 and had been thrown out of their home. Some had spent all their benefits on drugs and alcohol and asked us to refer them to the food bank, this was a request I never fulfilled and explained to them that buying food with benefits should be prioritised over alcohol and drugs.

Admittedly, there were unfortunate people who had to be referred to the food banks because of the bureaucracy of the welfare system or because they had just lost their job. Many criticise the government over food banks, but we need to look at ourselves as well. Billions of pounds' worth of food and over 7 million tonnes is wasted in the UK every year; enough to feed every homeless person three meals a day. Individuals and supermarkets have improved this in recent years but there is no magic bullet to address the usage of food banks.

The likes of Ken Loach and Owen Jones believe throwing more money at people in poverty helps them. Conversely I agree with the founder of the *Big Issue*, John Bird, who believes that a hand up is better than a hand out. A hand out encourages people to stay where they are and not progress, a hand up encourages people to stand on their own two feet and fulfil their potential.

Moving Forward: Moving to Contribution Based Welfare

Although I am extremely critical of large parts of the welfare state, I am a firm believer that we need one. We will always need to look after the needy and provide a safety net to those who have fallen on hard times. As I have shown earlier in this chapter, the public have lost confidence in the welfare system. This is why we need to move to a genuinely contributory system.

I propose to limit to inflation any increases in working age unemployment benefits except for those which are contribution based. This needs to be dramatically increased for those who have paid tax and National Insurance. We have come a long way from Beveridge's contribution based social insurance system of the 1940s. The welfare system is mainly non-contributory and has few conditions attached to claiming benefits. On too many occasions, the system now creates the conditions to live a decent life, and is no longer just a safety net for those in need. But when people do claim contributory benefits they must be shocked at what they receive because this is such a little amount.

I knew a man living in the hostel I worked at who was previously earning £50,000 a year and lost everything due to being made redundant, family breakdown and he became an alcoholic. Even after contributing tens of thousands of pounds in tax, he was entitled to less than £70 a week. In addition, this benefit stops after six months, if your partner has a job or if you have £16,000 in savings. This is a shocking way to treat those who have contributed into the system and is in stark contrast to the many substances misusers I spoke off earlier in the chapter.

The vast majority of countries in Europe have a contribution-based welfare system and we should follow suit. This would mean all foreign nationals waiting a certain qualifying time period before claiming benefits. When David Cameron asked the EU for permission to let us implement this, they offered him an extremely watered-down version.

This response alongside the fact that we couldn't even stop Child Benefit being sent to children who didn't even live in this country, showed a real loss of national sovereignty. Highly educated and skilled migrants clearly contribute far more to our economy than they take out but there are many low-skilled migrants who work in low-skilled jobs and therefore are entitled to in-work benefits. As we leave the EU there should be a qualifying period for benefits of five years, this should lead to more faith being placed in the British welfare system from its critics.

Lower Taxes Instead of Higher Welfare

We will always need a fair welfare system to those who pay for it as well as those who receive it. The easiest thing for the government to do would be to avoid welfare reform and let millions of people stay on benefits with no hope or requirement to look for employment. Under Labour this is what happened and the knock on effect has been a poverty of ambition for many children growing up under that decade.

Apart from the fact that Labour welfare spending was unsustainable, we should be aspiring to do so much more for the poorest in our society. Addressing the underlying causes of poverty such as family breakdown and lack of employment opportunities is a crucial starting point, rather than just throwing money at people and keeping them where they are.

Work should still be the best route out of poverty for both those who are unemployed and those who are on low incomes. The Conservatives have undoubtedly made tough decisions on welfare reform but this is to achieve the goal of a higher wage, low tax, lower welfare spending society. Alongside benefit freezes and further restrictions, a £1,000 a year tax cut as been introduced for basic rate taxpayers and more recently the living wage is being implemented as well as 30 hours' free childcare.

All these measures make it far more attractive to be in work but as stated in the Economy chapter, we should go further to help the lowest earners and ensure less welfare spending. If we can equalise the thresholds for both income tax and National Insurance this would put £500 a year in the pocket of the lowest earners.

Other measures I propose include lowering the living wage threshold to 21, cutting VAT on fuel bills which will help the poorest in society and reduce the need for welfare spending in the first place. Letting people keep more of their own money to begin with is the best way to trust people and encourage responsibility. Taking this money and then giving it back in government top ups creates a culture of dependency which in turn prohibits social mobility.

6 The Case Against Socialism

> *"Socialism is a philosophy of failure, the creed of ignorance, and the gospel of envy, its inherent virtue is the equal sharing of misery."*[55]
>
> *– Winston Churchill, 1948*

Introduction

I am still often met with dumbfounded looks when I tell people that I am a Conservative. Questions include: You seem so nice how can you be a Conservative? You don't come from a well-off family how can you be a Conservative? You've worked with the homeless, young unemployed and children in care how can you be a Conservative? What I respond with, is what I've felt for many years, I am instinctively against socialism as I believe in freedom. I believe in the values of responsibility, living within your means, hard work and freedom of the individual. I believe in a meritocratic society where people can go as far as their talents and hard work will let them, not a socialist society where hard work is punished as this results in widening inequality.

Equality of opportunity is why I am a Conservative; socialists believe in equality of outcome. Imagine a world where there is no incentive to work hard because you will be met with the same rewards as someone who does not wish

55 Winston Churchill, 1948.

to work. Or a world where there is no such thing as private property or enterprise as the government owns everything. People often say socialism or even communism sounds good in theory; I think it sounds terrifying.

As I have outlined, the Left are prejudice against Conservatives and automatically label us as 'nasty', 'elitist' and even 'evil'. They see themselves as morally superior but don't see the contradiction in this. If they were such moral people, they wouldn't be so aggressive and shout down anybody who disagrees with them.

However, I don't believe the Left have always been like this as there are many traditions of Old Labour I deeply respect. Even the modern day Blue Labour faction within the current Labour movement has great values of flag and family. Unfortunately, this is a tiny minority in the current Labour Party as they are now dominated by the *Guardian*-reading metropolitan elite. The middle class in the Labour movement now see the working class as an ungrateful hindrance and disdain at their patriotism.

Throughout this chapter I will use examples of how this has come about, especially under the leadership of Jeremy Corbyn. Culturally the Labour Party is divided in two and this coalition will ultimately crumble in the coming years; Brexit is just the tip of the iceberg. In my view, the current Labour Party has shown itself to be the real nasty party in the last few years, as the far Left have taken over and intend to begin an all-out class war on the rich.

Social mobility will be under attack if they gain power as by definition this concept creates inequality. This is why we need a Conservative Party who can take on and debate this socialist dogma, convincing the patriotic Labour supporters in the process that we can represent their interests.

Traditions of the Old Labour Party

In the nineteenth century it was clear that Britain needed a political party to represent the interests of the working class. With many still working in terrible conditions, long hours and poor pay, movements were created to campaign for the working class to receive the vote. Campaigners for the vote were outraged but also inspired by the Great Reform Act of 1832,[56] which gave much of the middle class the vote.

In 1838 the Chartist movement was set up and campaigned on issues such as universal suffrage, a secret ballot and no property qualifications to be able to stand as an MP. Inspirational working-class movements like the Chartists were made of people across the political spectrum from conservative to socialist. However, there is no doubt that movements like this were the precursor to the creation of the Labour movement at the end of the nineteenth century and the beginning of the twentieth century. Serious state intervention was clearly needed to improve the conditions of the working class.

Clement Attlee's government of 1945–51 is often cited as the greatest Labour Government. After six years of all-out war, the people wanted a country where the State would intervene. Labour radically expanded the welfare state and of course founded the National Health Service. It was undoubtedly a socialist government economically but a major part of its appeal was its patriotism and the prioritisation of security.

Attlee was probably the most modest prime minister of all time but he was a fierce patriot. He fought during World War One and was carried of the battlefield three times. His proudest act was to join Churchill's Coalition Government in 1940. It guaranteed the sort of cohesion and feeling of common purpose that was absent at the outset of the war. As

56 The Great Reform Act, 1832.

prime minister, Attlee was instrumental in setting up NATO and was convinced the atomic bomb was crucial for Britain's projection of power in the world. As well as a tough security policy, Attlee was socially conservative in many ways, believing in a strong family unit and controlled immigration.

Although Attlee was tough on security issues there is no getting away from the negative effects from the long-term economic record of his government. Creating the NHS and welfare state were great achievements but in doing so he dramatically increased public spending. This is not a bad thing in itself but the planned economy which was pursued included mass nationalisation of the commanding heights of industry. Such industries included the coal mines to railways to even Thomas Cook. Mass nationalisation was maintained under the post-war consensus for over 30 years until Margaret Thatcher's election to office.

The impact of nationalisation meant the economy stagnated compared to other nations who nicknamed Britain the 'sick man of Europe'. As well as nationalisation, food rationing was the other main plank to Attlee's economic policy. When World War Two ended, the Labour Party sought to continue food rationing indefinitely, while the Conservatives where against such extreme action. Food rationing under Attlee's Government was even more stringent than it was in World War Two. The 1951 General Election led to the Conservatives defeating Labour as they promised to end food rationing and at the same time keep popular institutions like the NHS.

Old and Current Values

Although I am extremely critical of Clement Attlee's economic policies, I see him as a representative of the values of many Old Labour supporters. Left-wing patriotism was at the heart of the Labour Party up until the 1970s and there still remains millions of patriotic Labour voters. They stand up for the national anthem, they believe in fair and managed immigration and they are tough on law and order. In addition to this they believe in a strong work ethic and two-parent families as the best way to raise children. They have no time for people who do not wish to work, who sneer at the monarchy, believe in uncontrolled immigration, destroying our nuclear weapon and sympathising with terrorists.

Such views are held by the majority of Labour's old working-class base and Brexit showed that they are now held in contempt by the metropolitan graduate class who now dominate the party. I have heard dozens of young middle-class Labour supporting graduates be dismayed at the fact that so many working-class people voted for Brexit. Stating things like: 'They are so uneducated, should they even have the vote?' 'There should be an IQ test for people to vote in elections'. 'I can't believe 17.4 million people in Britain are racist'. This is just several of the comments I've heard in the last year from graduate Labour insulting the less educated Labour voters. And yet because of the tribal nature of Labour's politics, many of the working-class voters astonishingly still vote for the party despite the sneering from the Corbynistas.

After analysing the traditional values of many Labour voters in the midlands and the north, it's now important to look at who's been running the party for the last 20 years. With Tony Blair moving the Labour Party to the centre ground he went out of his way to attract middle class supporters. This meant policies were introduced which alienated the old working-class base. In 2004, the most significant of these policies, was the decision to open the borders to the new eastern European countries who had joined the EU. This led to alienation amongst old Labour supporters as they have seen their community change beyond recognition and anyone who was against mass immigration was instantly branded a racist under New Labour. With people struggling to see a doctor, access social housing or send their child to a local school, the BNP increased in popularity during the New Labour years as many felt disenfranchised.

There is no better example of this than in the 2010 General Election campaign when Gordon Brown was caught on microphone calling lifelong Labour supporter, Gillian Duffy, 'a bigoted woman' because she dared to mention immigration. From Blair's landslide in 1997 to Brown's humiliation in 2010, New Labour lost 5 million voters during this period. In recent years the Labour Party membership and leadership have moved further away from their working-class base. As already stated they have been shouting down their voters for too long, especially in regards to the EU and immigration.

We saw this during the EU Referendum when the Labour MP Pat Glass was campaigning in Sawley, Derbyshire. After being asked a question about immigration and benefits, Pat Glass was afterwards caught on camera saying "The very first person I come to was a horrible racist. I'm never coming back to wherever this is". If you want to see what the Labour Party stands for today look at the leadership in the shadow cabinet. Jeremy Corbyn (Leader of the Opposition), John McDonnell (Shadow Chancellor), Emily Thornberry (Shadow Foreign Secretary) and Diane Abbott (Shadow Home Secretary). They are all London MPs and show contempt for the patriotic working classes in their own way. From Corbyn and McDonnell's cosy relationship with the IRA to Thornberry sneering at the English flag and tweeting about it, to Abbott's belief that anybody who believes immigration should come down is a racist. There is a huge cultural divide in the Labour Party's values which is not sustainable.

I decided to write this book as I am strong advocate of social mobility and I believe the Conservatives are the only party to achieve this. By definition socialists are against social mobility as it creates inequality. Socialism fails to give incentives for people to work their way up to be the best they can because it punishes aspiration. In a meritocratic society those who work hard are rewarded for their efforts. In recent years, Labour has defined themselves as being the anti-work party. They are against any caps on welfare spending and believe in unlimited benefits even if somebody is not fulfilling their obligations. They support the Southern Rail strikers who have cost commuters and the economy millions of pounds because they are striking over who opens the door on the trains.

In the 2015 Labour Leadership election I remember Blairite contender Liz Kendall saying that people had said to her on the doorstep that they 'couldn't support Labour because they worked'. What was the audience's response when they heard this? They groaned at her for daring to listen to the electorate. The Labour Party should change their name as the last thing they stand for are the labourers who are the backbone of this country. It is an astounding fact that every Labour Government in history has left unemployment higher than when it first came to office. I wish more young people knew this fact so they could revaluate whether a Labour Government would actually deliver them a better future.

Weakness on Security

If there is one thing that scares me more than the modern socialist's economic policies, it is their attitude when it comes to this country's security. During the 2015 Conservative Conference, David Cameron called out Jeremy Corbyn's 'Britain hating ideology'. The words may have been aggressive but he couldn't have been more right. Everything Corbyn has ever campaigned for shows that he believes the West are evil and everyone, including those who wish to harm our country, is a victim as a result of this. This has taken many forms including support for the IRA, Fidel Castro and sympathising with Hamas.

Let's take the IRA for example, during the 2017 General Election, Corbyn told a Question Time audience that he was not present at a commemoration which held a minute's silence just for IRA victims but he was there to commemorate all those who died in Northern Ireland. This simply wasn't true. Corbyn attended over 70 IRA backed events, marched at rallies with them and invited IRA leaders to Westminster in 1985 just several weeks after the Brighton Bomb (where the IRA attempted to assassinate the whole British cabinet including Margaret Thatcher). He claimed he attended such events to help with a peace agreement but even former SDLP leader Seamus Mallon said this was not the case. Corbyn never denounced the IRA in public during their bombing campaigns but was only too quick to denounce the British Army.

Corbyn did not speak to the unionist/loyalist side in Northern Ireland so there is no way he could claim to try to bring about peace in the region. The Shadow Chancellor John McDonnell went further in this support for the IRA, as in 2003 he spoke at an event honouring the IRA for their 'bombs and bullets strategy'.[57] I come from Northern Ireland and one of my earliest memories was being six years old when the Omagh bombing happened in 1998. Twenty-nine people died including a woman who was pregnant with twins – these comments should send a chill down the spine of anybody who is against terrorism.

When Fidel Castro died in November 2016 Corbyn stated "For all his flaws, he was a champion of social justice"[58] and Ken Livingstone commented "Initially he wasn't very good on lesbian and gay rights, but the key things that mattered was that people had a good education, good healthcare, and wealth was evenly distributed".[59] Despite all the claims from the Left that Britain has a biased media, I couldn't believe how lightly they got off.

Fidel Castro was a brutal dictator who killed tens of thousands of his own people and Corbyn was happy to overlook this because he was 'a champion for social justice'.

---

57 John McDonnell, 2003.
58 Jeremy Corbyn, November 2016.
59 *The Today Programme*, BBC Radio 4, 26th November 2016.

Is a man who puts on show trials and executes opponents a champion for social justice? Is a man who tortured and killed gay people a champion of social justice? Is a man who outlawed trade unions and killed supporters of democracy a champion of social justice? Even if funding was put into education, the young people in the schools were being brainwashed by the Communist State to worship Castro. But logically Corbyn's response makes perfect sense as Cuba was an original anti-Western, anti-business and anti-freedom nation. Corbyn and the far Left were happy to overlook the human and democratic rights violations because they espoused an anti-capitalist message.

As well as sympathy for brutal dictators and terrorist organisations, many socialists, such as the Stop the War Coalition (strangely named as they don't protest against Russia's wars), believe terrorist attacks on our country mean 'we reap the whirlwind of foreign policy intervention'.[60] First, let me give some of my own opinions on such foreign policy interventions. I think the 2003 Iraq war was completely unnecessary and we should never have invaded. I am also sceptical of the invasion of Afghanistan and Libya although I understand why we entered those countries. I am not some sort of right-wing warmonger who believes in our foreign interventions. I must say though; I am disgusted by much of the modern Left's views on our foreign policy. During the 2017 terror attacks in Manchester and London, Corbyn was the first to use these dreadful attacks for political gains. He spoke of foreign policy having an influence on terrorist attacks even though ISIS themselves have stated they would attack us even if we didn't go near the Middle East.

This is a ridiculous argument by Corbyn as the 2016 Brussels attacks and the 2017 Stockholm and Barcelona attacks target countries that had not been involved with any

60 https://www.ft.com/content/b249730a-4170-11e7-82b6-896b95f30f58 [Accessed 6th June 2017]

Middle Eastern wars. Corbyn has a long history of being anti-Western, stating he was against NATO and believes that ISIS supporters should "not be prosecuted for expressing a political view".[61]

The New 'Nasty Party'

The modern day Left are champions of social justice and equality for all... except if you're a Conservative or for that matter anywhere to the Right of Ed Millband, i.e. Blairites. Except if you're aspirational and seek to earn money and do well in life. Except if you are a 'Zionist' who condemn Hamas sending rockets into Israel. The modern day Labour member regards the Conservatives as the evil elitist enemy who need to be destroyed. From the perpetual protestors near Downing Street screaming 'Tories Out' (obviously not understanding how democracy works), to Owen Jones attacking the Conservatives for welfare reform and stating that those who come from private schools aren't allowed an opinion on the subject.

Who can forget the celebrations of these people at the death of Margaret Thatcher or what about the 2016 Labour Conference where 'Tories are vermin' mugs and t-shirts were being promoted? This is sheer nasty behaviour. More recently during the 2017 election, Captain Ska's 'Liar Liar' an unbelievably unbearable song showed how nasty the Left can be. They are meant to be kind, considerate, and tolerant but release a song called 'Liar Liar' which aims for character assassination and calls Conservatives 'fascists'. Or let's take John McDonnell's 'day of rage' in July 2017. Thousands of angry demonstrators screaming 'Tory Scum', some with placards showing Theresa May's head on a pike. The hypocrisy is rank. Conservative members think Labour are naive and economically illiterate, Labour members despise us.

---

61 Jeremy Corbyn, Parliamentary Debate, 15th December 2014.

Internal Labour divisions have been a constant theme since Jeremy Corbyn was elected in 2015. There has been a concerted effort to erase 'the cancerous growth of Blairites' from Labour's history. MPs and a new militant membership have been at war with each other. During the vote to bomb ISIS in December 2015, the membership sought to bully and harass MPs not to vote for the bombing. This led to death threats and protests outside MPs constituency offices. In addition to this, during the 2016 Labour Leadership challenge a brick was thrown through potential leadership contender Angela Eagle's constituency office and constituency party meetings were suspended because of the membership harassing each other. The scale of this division was underreported at the time.

Anti-Semitism has been another huge issue in Labour since Corbyn was elected. With Ken Livingstone leading the charge calling Hitler a Zionist and in 2016 it was reported over 50 labour members (including councillors and parliamentary candidates) had been suspended over anti-Semitism. This issue arose most recently during the 2017 General Election as *Women's Hour* presenter Emma Barnett was trolled on Twitter for being Jewish by pro-Corbyn supporters. When your leader has called Hamas 'friends', it gives these trolls licence to be anti-Semitic.

Election 2017: A Socialist Manifesto?

Labour's 2017 Manifesto is certainly of socialist ilk but I would argue it would merely be a starting point for Jeremy Corbyn and John McDonnell. If given the chance they undoubtedly would be much more radical in government. Speaking to many young people who support Corbyn they have no memory or historical knowledge of the 1970s when we last had socialism in action.

Many of them don't know anything about the three-day week, the unions governing Britain instead of the government, inflation over 20%, bodies left unburied and bins not being collected because of strikes. There is a reason why Britain was nicknamed the 'sick man of Europe' during these years. They don't remember the bullying and intimidation which took place in the Labour movement in the 1980s and their unelectable move to the Left. The likes of Jeremy Corbyn, John McDonnell, Diane Abbott, Ken Livingstone and Dennis Skinner pine for these days to return. What the young graduates who support Corbyn care about is the massive debts they have when they leave university, the difficulty to get secure employment and get on the housing ladder. After 30 years of the hated 'neo-liberalism', they are being offered easy solutions to complicated problems as the Left promise to spend the top 5% of earners' money for them.

Let's imagine Corbyn wins a General Election and is implementing his polices. What would happen during that five-year parliament? The 2020 General Election is won by Jeremy Corbyn with a majority of 50 (with a similar manifesto to 2017) against a weakened Conservative Party after the hard slog of Brexit. Seventy-five percent of young people support Corbyn as they had never had a chance to elect a socialist government.

John McDonnell's Emergency Budget of 2020 sets out 'a new bold radical socialist vision for the country', with all tax, benefit and public spending changes taking place the following month. Tuition fees would be abolished at a cost of £11 billion a year and £100 billion of student debt would be wiped out to 'free the young from debt'. Corporation tax would be raised from 19% to 26% over a two-year period. Income tax would be raised to 50p in the pound for anybody earning over £80,000 a year. Further measures include a financial tax on the city of London, 20:1 pay ratios would be introduced and so would an excessive pay levy to deal with inequality.

The living wage would be raised instantly from £9 to £11 an hour and businesses would be expected to shoulder the burden. All public sector pay would be increased by 5% and the wheels would be put in motion to nationalise water, rail, energy and Royal Mail. The NHS and social care would receive £50 billion a year more. The benefit cap would be abolished and all benefits would be uprated by 3%. Benefit sanctions would be abolished and so would Work Capability Assessments. Finally, a £250 billion National Investment Fund would be created through an enormous increase in borrowing.

Where would we be in 2025 after five years of a radically socialist Labour Government? Corbyn achieves his core aim and creates a drastically more equal society, unfortunately it is an equally poor one. With huge tax rises on corporations, income tax, a financial tax, and pay ratios, it raises the expected £50 billion in the first year and all seems well.

However, the financially mobile elite and business investors simply move to Paris and New York as presidents Macron and Trump are cutting taxes there. From digital giants Google to premier league footballers, they move to countries where they can keep more of their own money. After raising £50 billion from these higher taxes on the wealthy in 2021, this falls to a mere £5 billion in 2022 and by 2024 the government is losing £10 billion a year rather than raising £50 billion. After the implementation of a £11 minimum wage (rising to £15 by 2025), unemployment stands at 4 million people and food banks are more widespread than ever.

The promises on the NHS, social care, childcare, schools, tuition fees, nationalisation, benefits and pensions leaves Chancellor McDonnell in quite the predicament. By 2023 (after a year of recession) the government has a higher budget deficit than after the financial crash of 2008 and is forced to raise income tax, National Insurance and VAT on ordinary taxpayers. Social mobility has collapsed as jobs are scarce, taxes soar so it pays more to be on benefits and aspiration is discouraged as it creates the great evil of inequality. Five years of a truly socialist Labour Government has achieved the goal of a more equal society, but a much poorer one with much less money for public services.

Conclusion: The Next Conservative Government

The 2017 General Election showed that many young people are rejecting Conservatism and instead are turning to Jeremy Corbyn's Labour Party. If the Conservative Party are to combat the growing tide of socialism in Britain today, we need to immediately improve our Party image and deepen this change with new policy proposals. Setting out what we stand for, not just what we are against is of utmost importance in the coming years.

Instead of running away from the debate with Labour, we need to take them on with pro-capitalist arguments, but why should young people support capitalism if they have no capital? Corbyn has tapped into genuine concerns over affordability of housing, student debt and excessive pay for the wealthy. We need to show that his policy solutions would destroy the life chances of the many, not the few. We need to take on the ideology of socialism, which punishes aspiration and is against the very idea of owning property.

Let's now imagine the Conservatives defeat Corbyn's Labour at the 2020 General Election. In the ensuing years how do we go about creating a truly meritocratic society and give a radical Tory vision of where we would like the country to be? We need to save this country from a Corbyn Government but we can only do this by offering an inspiring alternative.

During the period between the elections of 2017 and 2020, the Conservatives finally wake up to the urgent matter of a need for rebranding. Once and for all, the Party dispel its reputation of being 'elitist, nasty and arrogant'. Critical steps are made to modernise the Party and ensure it looks more like the country it seeks to represent. The goal of building a mass membership is reached which rivals the Labour Party as structures and policies are democratised. Under a down to earth bold leadership, the membership is given an authentic say on Party policy and the conference is opened up to undecided voters. Open primaries are introduced which give non-Tory members the chance to pick candidates who are charismatic and have independent personalities.

The traditional and the modern voter are both targeted by a communication strategy which embraces town hall debates but also social media platforms. The stage-managed events of the past are scrapped in favour of open debate, taking on Labour face to face. The Conservatives logo is changed from a tree to ladder to make it more relevant to would be voters. There is a public campaign by the leadership to spread the word of this change. The ladder signals aspiration and opportunity which is the very definition of what the Conservatives believe, which is a truly meritocratic Britain where hard work and talent prevails. Against all expectations, on Thursday 7th May 2020 the Conservatives are elected with a majority of 50. The Party's image has changed, but what policies in government will entrench this new found public popularity?

Victory in the 2020 General Election is partly due to a change in image, but also to do with a bold vision for Britain. The 2020 Manifesto's front cover promises to build a more socially mobile society and promises to build an economy that eradicates 'unfair' inequalities, promoting opportunities for all. With a free trade deal secured with the EU and the budget deficit at minimal levels, bold reforms can now take place.

The first Budget in the new government is hailed a 'Tory Budget for low earners'. With a confirmation that the living wage will rise from £9 in 2020 to £12 by 2025. Lowering the age from 25 to 21 is introduced to help support the young. Tax cuts for the lowest earners are prioritised. Over a three-year period, National Insurance and income tax thresholds will merge, resulting in a £500 a year tax cut for low and middle earners. Tory tax cuts are further enhanced as the best way to redistribute wealth as the new found freedom from the EU means that VAT will be scrapped on all fuel, saving low and middle earners hundreds of pounds in energy and petrol bills. From the government's first Budget, the public can see that bold Tory tax cuts are a much better way to help the just about managing, rather than increased welfare dependency.

Once again the Party begins to use the phrase 'popular capitalism' and vows to give young people hope in owning a property of their own. The government recognise that the realistic chance of owning capital is imperative in a capitalist society and a national drive is needed to tackle both the supply and demand. As home ownership has plummeted during the last 30 years, the Party recognise this could lead to an existential crisis for the British dream.

By following the Conservative prime minister Harold MacMillan's lead, 300,000 homes a year are to be built. This will take several years to reach and in the meantime the government follow through with banning agency fees and extending the Lifetime ISA so young people can be given a helping hand onto the property ladder. The latter is made more generous by promising a top of 50% of what young people save. This means if a person under 40 saves £8,000 for a deposit, then the government will top this up with £4,000. Addressing the supply and demand side of housing means for the first time in a generation, home ownership amongst young people will increase over the term of the parliament.

Showing ways to pay for these changes are also important as every Conservative government promotes fiscal responsibility. Stamp duty is doubled for those homes bought for over £10 million, a significant revenue raiser aiming to target billionaire foreign oligarchs. An extra Council Tax band is introduced on the most expensive 5% of homes. Finally, inheritance tax is made more progressive by raising the threshold to £1.5 million, but raising it on estates worth more than this. It is emphasised that these policy changes show the public that the Conservatives do not believe in widening inequality but at the same time do not intend to damage aspiration. Only taxing the most expensive properties is a far cry from Labour's damaging plans to raise taxes on income and businesses.

The new Conservative Government understand that too often the public's perception is that we are on not on their side, but on the side of the big corporations and those avoiding tax. Moving forward, the government recognise that an even playing field is imperative in promoting growth which funds our public services. Keeping corporation tax low is crucial to remain competitive as an economy but the government now intends to do more to support the backbone of our economy, the small business owner. Introducing a cut in business rates is announced, helping create more jobs and add extra much needed dynamism to the high street.

Helping the self-employed in the so-called gig economy is also prioritised, showing we are on the side of those who may be exploited by businesses. This means extending workers' rights so that those who work for the likes of Uber or Deliveroo legally need to receive holiday pay and other workers' rights. At the same time, the new government intends to even the playing field between small and large businesses, by making sure all big businesses pay their fair share of tax and do not reward failure. With corporation tax being reduced from 29% in 2010 to 17% by 2019, big businesses cannot complain they are being treated unfairly by the Conservatives. But this lower tax-friendly environment means the government can be even tougher on those not paying their fair share of tax. The diverted profit tax is to be frequently used if big businesses avoid tax, this means a 25% tax on their profit if HMRC suspect them of foul play. High pay is also targeted by the new government but in a pro-capitalist non-damaging way. Crony capitalism is to be eradicated by giving shareholders more powers to veto executive pay. Some within business howl at this policy but the vast majority of businesses and shareholders see this as a pro-capitalist measure.

By 2020, the 2010 Coalition Government's school reforms is a factor that is contributing to a rise in social mobility. Extra money for the poorest pupils has been sustained to help close the attainment gap. Doubling Pupil Premium money for the early years is a long-term investment for the new government. In addition to the Pupil Premium, the new Government is to invest further in our schools and to raise aspirations. This means extra funding to bring back career advice, digital, financial and business classes and extra training to combat the scourge of mental health issues.

Focusing particularly on the poorest pupils, bold decisions are made by the new Education Secretary to help the most disadvantaged become more socially mobile. This includes the creation of a new type of grammar school but with strict rules so it focusses exclusively on the most disadvantaged. New rules are introduced, that only allow grammars to open in areas that have the lowest 20% performing local authorities and almost exclusively only allowing those from low incomes to attend. This challenges many on the Right who are against such stringent rules but social mobility must be the key priority. To further tackle the attainment gap in the bottom 20% of areas, teachers are given a 15% pay rise to be incentivised to work in these schools.

The most difficult group to persuade to switch from Corbyn to Conservative has been university students and graduates.

With Corbyn promising to scrap tuition fees the Conservatives match this pledge but instead propose to introduce a graduate tax. From 2022, new university graduates will instead pay a tax instead of paying back a loan. Instead of paying back 9% of earnings after reaching £25,000 it is made more progressive as the graduate tax means paying back 7% after reaching £27,000. With this policy proposal, the Conservatives show they are listening but continue to argue that those graduates who go on to earn more than £27,000 should pay something back and not expect others to fit the bill. In a progressive move, the graduate tax is raised to 10% on those earning more than £75,000. Tuition fees are kept for foreign students but the new government are determined for the best and the brightest to come and work in Britain. As a result, students from overseas are taken out of the immigration figures with little opposition.

New legislation is introduced to ensure Russell Group universities take more of the most disadvantaged young people. In a move to help graduates, grants are offered to those who seek unpaid internships but do not have a means to pay. All these policy measures put together help make inroads into Labour's big lead on young people and graduates when it comes to voting.

With a higher wage and tax cuts saving the lowest paid hundreds of pounds a year, the Conservative Government feel they have the scope to promote stable families and reduce welfare dependency. A revolution in responsibility is called for by the government and the Troubled Families Programme is extended. This focuses on the most troubled 5% of families and will offer extensive help from charities and local authorities. This means extra supports to ensure truancy does not happen, parents are in work and reoffending does not occur.

Millions more from the Big Lottery is released to help fund charities and volunteering is promoted more than ever before.

With students, working people, job seekers and pensioners all volunteering at record levels, the nation is becoming at ease with itself. Communities celebrate the joys of immigration but unskilled immigration is controlled to sustainable levels. Welfare is seen to be fair as it is reformed to make it primarily contribution based. This decreases scepticism of welfare, as the public are reassured that those who put in can get more out when they fall on hard times.

The policies introduced by the Conservative Government between 2020 and 2025, have guaranteed the Party's future and changed Britain for the better. Instead of stale and bland rhetoric, the Conservatives introduce long-lasting progressive polices which has dramatically increased social mobility in Britain.

The economy has been reformed but in a Tory way which cuts taxes for the lowest earners, moving away from in-work benefits. Businesses are created like never before as taxes are cut and an even playing field is established between small businesses and multinational corporations. Investment in housing has led to an increase in home ownership and popular capitalism is back with a bang. Young people from the poorest backgrounds are given the chance to go to the best schools and will no longer have student debt when they leave university. Unfair inequality has been reduced, social mobility has been increased and strong family units are promoted. For the first time, Britain is moving towards a classless society where there is opportunity for all who work hard for it.